Thinking Critically: Biofuels

William Dudley

ReferencePoint
Press®

San Diego, CA

© 2016 ReferencePoint Press, Inc.
Printed in the United States

For more information, contact:
ReferencePoint Press, Inc.
PO Box 27779
San Diego, CA 92198
www.ReferencePointPress.com

Picture Credits:
Maury Aaseng: 8, 17, 22, 30, 36, 43, 49, 57, 63

LIBRARY OF CONGRESS CATALOGING-IN-PUBLICATION DATA

Dudley, William, 1964–
    Thinking critically : Biofuels / by William Dudley.
        pages cm. -- (Thinking critically)
    Audience: Grade 9 to 12.
    Includes bibliographical references and index.
    ISBN 978-1-60152-816-2 (hardback) -- ISBN 1-60152-816-7 (hardback) 1. Biomass energy--Juvenile literature. I. Title.
    TP339.D83   2016
    662'.88--dc23
                                                                    2015007512

Contents

Foreword

"Literacy is the most basic currency of the knowledge economy we're living in today." Barack Obama (at the time a senator from Illinois) spoke these words during a 2005 speech before the American Library Association. One question raised by this statement is: What does it mean to be a literate person in the twenty-first century?

E.D. Hirsch Jr., author of *Cultural Literacy: What Every American Needs to Know*, answers the question this way: "To be culturally literate is to possess the basic information needed to thrive in the modern world. The breadth of the information is great, extending over the major domains of human activity from sports to science."

But literacy in the twenty-first century goes beyond the accumulation of knowledge gained through study and experience and expanded over time. Now more than ever literacy requires the ability to sift through and evaluate vast amounts of information and, as the authors of the Common Core State Standards state, to "demonstrate the cogent reasoning and use of evidence that is essential to both private deliberation and responsible citizenship in a democratic republic."

The *Thinking Critically* series challenges students to become discerning readers, to think independently, and to engage and develop their skills as critical thinkers. Through a narrative-driven, pro/con format, the series introduces students to the complex issues that dominate public discourse—topics such as gun control and violence, social networking, and medical marijuana. All chapters revolve around a single, pointed question such as Can Stronger Gun Control Measures Prevent Mass Shootings?, or Does Social Networking Benefit Society?, or Should Medical Marijuana Be Legalized? This inquiry-based approach introduces student researchers to core issues and concerns on a given topic. Each chapter includes one part that argues the affirmative and one part that argues the negative—all written by a single author. With the single-author format the predominant arguments for and against an issue can be synthesized into clear, accessible discussions supported by details and evidence including relevant facts, direct quotes, current examples, and statistical illustrations. All volumes include focus questions to guide students as they read each pro/con discussion, a list of key facts, and an annotated list of related organizations and websites for conducting further research.

The authors of the Common Core State Standards have set out the particular qualities that a literate person in the twenty-first century must have. These include the ability to think independently, establish a base of knowledge across a wide range of subjects, engage in open-minded but discerning reading and listening, know how to use and evaluate evidence, and appreciate and understand diverse perspectives. The new *Thinking Critically* series supports these goals by providing a solid introduction to the study of pro/con issues.

Biofuels

In July 2012 an aircraft carrier strike group of five US Navy ships performed a series of military exercises in the Pacific Ocean. Their maneuvers were largely routine but for one thing—the ships and airplanes were powered by a 50/50 blend of petroleum-based marine diesel or jet fuel mixed with 450,000 gallons (1.7 million L) of biofuel produced from algae, used cooking oil, chicken fat, and other nonpetroleum sources. The military exercise demonstrated that biofuels made from nontraditional sources are feasible without expensive engine retrofits. Biofuels work "in the engines that we have, in the aircraft that we have . . . in the ships that we have,"[1] said Secretary of the Navy Ray Mabus. The exercise, called the Great Green Fleet, represents just one step in an ambitious program to develop alternative fuels and to cut by half the navy's dependence on fuel from oil by 2020.

Not everyone was enthused by the navy's push for biofuels, especially when it was revealed that the biofuels used by the Great Green Fleet cost more than $26 a gallon. That figure was almost eight times higher than the $3.50 per gallon spent on conventional petroleum fuels. Critics in Congress said that spending such money on biofuels was foolish at a time when the Pentagon was facing serious budget and personnel cutbacks. Representative Mike Conaway of Texas introduced legislation that would restrict the navy's ability to procure more expensive biofuels. "We just want to require the Department of Defense to do exactly what every other American does when they buy fuel; they try to get the best price they can."[2]

The debate over navy fuel symbolizes much of the general public-policy debate over biofuels. Biofuels—fuels derived from cultivated crops such as corn and algae—can theoretically substitute for fossil fuels such as petroleum. Biofuels are already in use, although not nearly at the level of fossil fuels. For instance, ethanol made from US-grown corn provided 5.7 percent of America's transportation fuel consumption in 2012. Biofuels are expected to play an even greater role in the not-too-distant future. The International Energy Agency, for instance, has projected that biofuels may provide up to 27 percent of the world's transportation fuel needs by the year 2050. But questions have been raised on whether biofuels are worth the extra effort and expense associated with them, and whether they are truly a viable replacement for fossil fuels.

What Are Biofuels?

Biofuels are simply fuels (materials burned for energy) that are made out of organic matter, or biomass. Biomass sources for fuel can be plants such as corn or sugarcane that are cultivated and harvested for the express purpose of making fuel. Biofuels also can be developed from waste sources such as animal manure, used vegetable oil, sewage, or leftover wood from lumber operations. Depending on the source material, transforming raw organic material into usable biofuels often requires significant processing and engineering.

Biofuels can be solid, liquid, or gas. The wood used in fireplaces is technically biofuel. Indeed, several electric utilities in Europe use wood pellets as a fuel source. In the United States operators of coal-fired power plants have attempted to supplement or replace coal with wood. Gaseous forms of biofuels include methane, which is produced from animal manure. However, biofuels are probably most associated with liquid forms of fuel that are used to power automobiles, airplanes, and other vehicles. The most popular liquid biofuels in use at present are ethanol and biodiesel.

Ethanol and Other Liquid Biofuels

Ethanol is an alcohol liquid that is most commonly made from corn or sugarcane. Ethanol also can be made from sorghum, sugar beets, and

Biofuels: Incentives and Mandates

Many states have laws and regulations that promote the use of biofuels, including biodiesel and ethanol. These laws and regulations essentially fall into three categories. The first is financial incentives such as tax credits, tax exemptions, reduced tax rates, grants, loans, and funds. The second category involves vehicle acquisition and fuel use requirements. These mandate states, schools, and public fleets to acquire alternative fuel vehicles that run on biofuels, or use a certain percentage of biofuels. The third category, fuel standards and mandates, requires the use of low-carbon fuels and fuel blends.

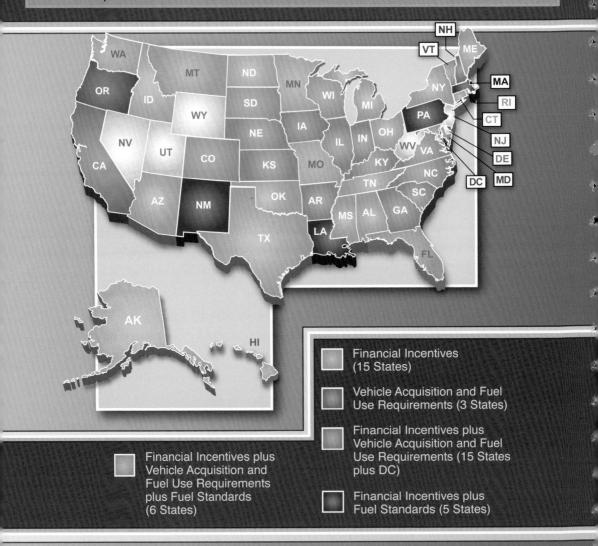

Financial Incentives (15 States)

Vehicle Acquisition and Fuel Use Requirements (3 States)

Financial Incentives plus Vehicle Acquisition and Fuel Use Requirements (15 States plus DC)

Financial Incentives plus Vehicle Acquisition and Fuel Use Requirements plus Fuel Standards (6 States)

Financial Incentives plus Fuel Standards (5 States)

Source: Center for Climate and Energy Solutions, "Biofuels: Incentives and Mandates." www.c2es.org.

sunflowers. A combination of fermentation, chemical processes, and heat breaks down the starches and sugars in the corn or other biomass source into usable fuel that is usually blended with gasoline.

Most ethanol production facilities use only the parts of the plant that are rich in sugars or starches, such as corn kernels. Scientists have long sought ways to use the rest of the plant (such as leaves and stalks) in order to make the whole process of biofuels production more efficient and environmentally sustainable. A challenge is that much of the organic material in the leaves and stalks is in the form of cellulose, the rigid material that makes plant cell walls. Cellulose is far more difficult to transform into biofuels than are starches. The science of converting starches into ethanol is well established; the science of converting cellulose into ethanol in an economically viable way is still in the research-and-development phase.

Biodiesel fuel, usable in diesel engines, is generally made by combining methanol (another form of alcohol) with vegetable oil or animal fat. Feedstock sources for biodiesel include palm oil, used cooking oil from restaurants, and algae. Seventy percent of global biodiesel production is situated in Europe.

Government Support for Biofuels

US production of biofuels has increased greatly in recent years, in large part because of state and federal policies. Such policies include business tax credits to encourage biofuels production and to lower consumer prices, requirements that government fleet vehicles run on biofuels, restrictions on importing biofuels (to encourage domestic production), and research grants to stimulate development of new biofuels technologies. Many of the tax credits and other programs have been phased out, but one important mechanism remains. The Renewable Fuels Standard (RFS) was created by federal legislation in 2007 and is administered by the Environmental Protection Agency. It mandates that a minimum volume of fuel used for transportation purposes in the United States consist of biofuels, regardless of their cost. In 2010, for example, the RFS required that almost 13 billion gallons (49 billion L) of biofuels such as ethanol and biodiesel be used either in pure form or blended with gasoline. That number rose steadily in subsequent years, reaching 36 billion gallons (136 billion L) in 2011. The RFS subsidizes and encourages producers of biofuels and source crops by guaranteeing a market for them. Other countries have instituted similar programs and mandates. In 2014 the European Union established a target that 27 percent of its energy consumption would come from renewable sources, including biofuels.

Largely as a result of the RFS and other government programs, the production of biofuels in the United States has grown 600 percent since the early 2000s. As of 2014 ethanol makes up 10 percent of the gasoline available in US filling stations. Similar trends can be seen in other parts of the world. The global production of biodiesel has risen from less than a billion liters (264 million gal) in 2000 to 21.4 billion liters (5.6 billion gal) in 2011.

Why Promote Biofuels?

Promoters of biofuels offer several reasons why they believe development of these fuels should be supported and why they are more advantageous than fossil fuels. Biofuels can help countries such as the United States become more self-sufficient in producing the energy they consume. Promoting biofuels can reduce America's reliance on foreign nations for its energy needs. This is considered important because many of these nations are located in politically volatile regions. Another advantage is that biofuels are a renewable source of energy. Corn and other plants can be grown year after year to replace the biomass used to make biofuels. Fossil fuels, by contrast, are not renewable; once they are extracted and burned, they are gone.

Perhaps the most significant driver of biofuels promotion is concern over carbon pollution. Burning fossil fuels releases carbon dioxide into the atmosphere; scientists estimate that the earth's atmosphere may contain 25 percent more carbon dioxide than it held before the Industrial Revolution. Increased concentrations of carbon dioxide and other so-called greenhouse gases released by fossil-fuel consumption are linked with potentially deleterious changes to the earth's climate and oceans. These include rising sea levels, coastal flooding, and more severe hurricanes, droughts, and other weather events. Concerns over carbon pollution and climate change have led countries to commit via international treaties to reduce their carbon emissions. The United States, for instance, has pledged to reduce its greenhouse gas (GHG) emissions by 17 percent below 2005 levels by the year 2020. This has led to searches for sources of energy other than fossil fuels.

Biofuels and Greenhouse Gas Emissions

Biofuels have emerged as a possible, but controversial, method of reducing the amount of carbon pollution placed in the earth's atmosphere. While burning biofuels such as ethanol releases carbon pollution to the atmosphere just like fossil fuels, the process of making those biofuels, including growing the plants that produce them, takes carbon out of the atmosphere. Bliss Baker of the Global Renewable Fuels Alliance asserts that "biofuels like ethanol are the only cost-effective and commercially available alternative to crude oil and are proven to reduce harmful GHG emissions and help in the fight against climate change."[3]

However, carbon pollution abatement and other claimed environmental benefits of biofuels have been questioned by a growing number of environmentalist organizations, including the Environmental Working Group (EWG). They are especially critical of

> "Many scientists now question the environmental benefit of so-called biofuels."[4]
>
> —Environmental Working Group, an environmentalist group that opposes biofuels.

policies encouraging the use of food crops such as corn for biofuels, arguing that dedicating more land for crop cultivation actually increases carbon emissions in the atmosphere. A 2012 study estimated that farmers

11

in the American Midwest converted 8 million acres (3 million ha) of grasslands and wetlands into cornfields, resulting in millions of tons of new greenhouse gas emissions in the atmosphere. "In light of these emissions," concludes the EWG, "many scientists now question the environmental benefit of so-called biofuels produced by converting food crops."[4] Supporters of biofuels argue that new technologies and feedstock sources can enable them to fulfill their promise of environmentally clean energy. Biofuels will continue to occupy an important role in upcoming debates over energy sources and climate change.

Chapter One

Should the US Government Continue to Support Ethanol Production?

The US Government Should Support Ethanol Production

- Government supports such as the Renewable Fuel Standard have greatly increased ethanol production.
- Ethanol production has reduced America's dependency on foreign sources of oil.
- Ethanol support has strengthened America's farm economy and has benefited rural communities.
- Ethanol production can help reduce total greenhouse gas emissions.

The Debate at a Glance

America's Ethanol Program Is Wasteful and Unworkable

- Ethanol programs cost taxpayers and consumers billions of dollars.
- Ethanol is an inferior fuel that corrodes engines and has worse fuel economy than gasoline or diesel.
- Ethanol production has little impact on America's energy security.
- Increased ethanol production has negative environmental consequences.

The US Government Should Support Ethanol Production

"U.S. ethanol . . . offers our nation's motorists a cost-saving, American-made, environmentally-friendly alternative to foreign oil, as well as a pathway to the next generation of biofuels."

—Bob Dinneen, president and chief executive officer of the Renewable Fuels Association.

Bob Dinneen, "Professor Flunks Ethanol 101," Renewable Fuels Association, January 18, 2013. www.ethanolrfa.org.

Consider these questions as you read:

1. What benchmarks are used to argue that ethanol programs are a success story? Are there other benchmarks that should be considered?
2. Many of the people who support ethanol fuels work in or represent the ethanol industry. Is this a factor that should affect whether one accepts their arguments? Why or why not?
3. What argument is made in response to the idea that, instead of corn ethanol, other more advanced biofuels should be promoted?

Editor's note: The discussion that follows presents common arguments made in support of this perspective, reinforced by facts, quotes, and examples taken from various sources.

The US corn ethanol industry is an American success story of both private innovation and bipartisan public policy. Ethanol, a grain alcohol that can be blended with gasoline, has become a major source of transportation fuel. Production of corn ethanol has grown from 1.6 billion gallons (6 billion L) in 2000 to more than 13 billion gallons (49 billion L) in 2013. Much of the credit for that growth goes to federal programs, especially the Renewable Fuels Standard (RFS). The RFS gives the federal government authority to mandate that refineries use certain amounts of ethanol and other biofuels in their gasoline and other products. The RFS and corn-based ethanol have both come under criticism in recent years, especially from the oil and gas industry, but their benefits to American society cannot be denied.

John R. Block, who served as secretary of agriculture under President Ronald Reagan, identifies three policy objectives of the RFS when it was expanded in 2007. These goals were increasing US energy security, helping US farmers, and driving innovation for new forms of biofuels. "First and foremost," he argues, "the program was intended to enhance U.S. energy security by displacing imported petroleum and diversifying the transportation fuels market." A second important goal, Block states, was to help farmers and the rural economy in general "by adding value to agricultural commodities"[5]—in other words, enabling farmers to sell their crops for higher prices. Finally, it was hoped that government support would spur private company innovation and create new technologies to produce more-advanced biofuels from plants other than corn. Block argues that the RFS has succeeded in all three policy objectives, that these objectives are still valuable, and that federal supports for ethanol should be continued.

Energy Security

Corn ethanol enhances America's energy security by helping the United States become more self-sufficient. America's dependence on foreign fossil fuel supplies has long been recognized as a challenge that needed solving. Oil price shocks created by foreign oil exporters have had devastating impacts for America's economy. Much of America's military policy is focused on securing oil supplies and oil shipping routes. America's security is also affected by the billions of dollars the United States spends each year to buy oil from foreign nations, many of which have agendas hostile to the United States. "These countries know we need their oil, and that reduces our influence, our ability to keep the peace in some areas," former president George W. Bush noted in a 2006 speech. "And so energy supply is a matter of national security."[6]

Corn-based ethanol has helped America reduce its dangerous dependence on foreign oil. By 2011 ethanol was replacing 10 percent of conventional gasoline in America's cars. Production of ethanol has increased from 250,000 barrels a day in 2005 to 870,000 barrels a day in 2013. This has helped reduce US fuel imports. From their 2005 peak of 308 million barrels a month, crude oil imports dropped 24 percent to 235 million barrels a month in 2013. Farmer and ethanol supporter Pam Johnson writes that reduced oil imports mean "money that would otherwise enrich dangerous nations abroad is creating jobs here in the United States."[7]

An Economic Boost

These American jobs are evidence that Block's second objective—helping America's farm economy—is being met. The RFS and related programs have, according to Block, "catalyzed an economic renaissance in the agriculture sector"[8] by driving investment in ethanol production and increasing net farm incomes. Whereas farmers benefit from bigger markets and higher crop prices, rural communities benefit from local jobs. Delayne Johnson, chief executive officer of an ethanol production company in Iowa, argues that "a typical U.S. ethanol plant supports nearly 3,000 jobs—not just at the production point itself, but also in transportation, equipment production and maintenance, and other sectors."[9] Johnson calculates that nearly 400,000 jobs in all are created or supported by US government policies on ethanol.

> "A typical U.S. ethanol plant supports nearly 3,000 jobs."[9]
>
> —Delayne Johnson, chief executive officer of Quad County Corn Processors in Galvia, Iowa.

Ethanol's Environmental Benefits

Ethanol creates more jobs and produces less pollution than gasoline. Ethanol has more oxygen in its formula than pure gasoline, making for a more complete combustion that produces fewer tailpipe emissions of nitrogen oxides, carbon monoxide, and compounds that produce ozone. Ethanol has largely replaced benzene and MTBE, fossil fuel–derived ad-

Government Mandates Have Boosted Ethanol Production

For many reasons, including energy security and long-term health of the environment, the United States must divert its energy sources. One important way to do that is for the government to promote the use of biofuels. To achieve this goal, federal legislation passed in 2007 mandated that a certain percentage of America's transportation fuel consist of corn-based ethanol. The effectiveness of the mandate can be seen in the sharp increase in ethanol production since 2007.

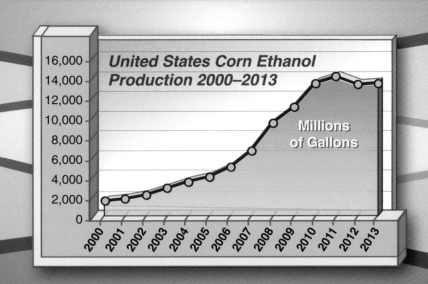

United States Corn Ethanol Production 2000–2013

Millions of Gallons

Source: Renewable Fuels Association, "Statistics," 2015. www.ethanolrfa.org.

ditives that have been linked to cancer and groundwater contamination. "Compared to most petroleum based fuels and additives," writes the Saskatchewan Eco Network, "ethanol is relatively non-toxic. It is completely biodegradable and poses little threat to groundwater sources."[10]

Ethanol also helps in the challenge of reducing carbon dioxide, methane, and other greenhouse gases that may contribute to significant long-term problems with the earth's climate. Burning fossil fuels releases carbon dioxide and other greenhouse gases into the atmosphere. Burning ethanol also releases carbon dioxide, but making that ethanol involves growing corn, which absorbs carbon dioxide from the atmosphere. The net result is that producing and burning ethanol has fewer total greenhouse gas emissions than producing and burning petroleum-based gasoline. A US Department of Energy study calculated that corn-based ethanol produces 34 percent less greenhouse gas emissions than does gasoline. According to the Renewable Fuels Association, "In 2013, the 13.3 billion gallons [50 billion L] of ethanol produced reduced greenhouse gas emissions from on-road vehicles by 38 million metric tons [41.8 million]." It adds that this is an amount "equivalent to removing 8 million cars from the road."[11]

Ethanol and Food Production

Critics of ethanol often claim that farmers should grow food, not fuel. They believe that government mandates for ethanol harm consumers by effectively displacing food production and driving up food prices. This is misleading. Ethanol is not produced from the sweet corn that humans eat. It is instead made from a strain of corn that is indigestible for humans and is used mostly as livestock feed. And even after the corn is processed into ethanol, its food value is not lost. Producing ethanol out of corn produces as a by-product something called Distiller's Dried Grains (DDGs). These contain the protein, fiber, and nutrients of the corn; many believe DDGs are a superior livestock feed than just corn itself.

Ethanol programs also should not be blamed for higher food prices. Commodities such as corn account for only 14 percent of the cost of groceries in the United States, and since 2007 there has been no discernable correlation between corn commodity prices and retail food prices. Food prices have remained relatively stable even as the RFS has greatly stimulated corn ethanol production.

The Next Generation of Biofuels

The United States is at an important turning point on the quest to develop biofuels. So-called first-generation biofuels are made from starchy crops such as corn or sugarcane. Thanks to government support, the United States has almost met its goal of 16 billion gallons (60.5 billion L) in annual production of first-generation biofuels. The next step is to encourage investment in developing the ability to make ethanol (and other biofuels) out of cellulose and other nonedible plant materials and crops, such as cornstalks and switchgrass. These advanced biofuels promise to be even more energy efficient and environmentally friendly than corn ethanol. The RFS does include mandates for the production and use of alternative biofuels in addition to corn ethanol.

Some critics of corn ethanol believe that America should instead support research and development of other biofuels. What they fail to realize is that the best way forward is to build on the foundation and investments already made by America's corn ethanol industry because of US government policies. "If we stay the course," argues chemistry professor Bruce Dale, "this second-generation biofuel industry can grow rapidly, providing energy security, environmental benefits, and the many other social and economic benefits that accompany energy consumption. However, a stable policy environment is required before a large second-generation biofuel industry can emerge."[12] In other words, pulling the plug on the federal government's support of ethanol, including the RFS, may well kill off private investment into ethanol and jeopardize the emergence of newer, cleaner biofuels. America's energy future is best secured by continuing the country's successful policies in supporting ethanol and other biofuels.

America's Ethanol Program Is Wasteful and Unworkable

"How did we reach the point where the government is promoting a dreadful fuel that gets worse fuel economy than gasoline or diesel, drives up food prices, damages car engines and has unintended environmental consequences?"

—Mark J. Perry, an economics professor at the University of Michigan–Flint.

Mark J. Perry, "Con: Renewable Fuels Standard Subsidies Unneeded as Sales of Cleaner Vehicles Surge," *GazetteXtra*, October 24, 2013. www.gazettextra.com.

Consider these questions as you read:

1. Do you believe the development of ethanol is worth any extra costs passed down to consumers purchasing fuel and food? How much cost per person do you think would be fair? Explain your answer.
2. Based on the facts and ideas presented in the discussion, do supporters and opponents of corn ethanol share the same general policy goals? If so, what accounts for their differing views on ethanol? If not, how do their goals differ?
3. The group Taxpayers for Common Sense, in addition to opposing the RFS, also opposes government tax breaks for oil drilling and the oil industry. Does this lend more credence to their anti-ethanol arguments? Why or why not?

Editor's note: The discussion that follows presents common arguments made in support of this perspective, reinforced by facts, quotes, and examples taken from various sources.

For the past decade and more, the federal government has provided lavish subsidies for the production of corn ethanol. These subsidies have benefited some farmers and ethanol producers, but their broader public value is questionable. "Through federal tax credits, loan guarantees, grants and other subsidies, billions of taxpayer dollars have been squandered on an industry that relentlessly seeks additional special interest carve-outs,"[13] writes Ryan Alexander, president of the advocacy group Taxpayers for Common Sense. Whereas some of the direct payments and credits for ethanol programs have been phased out by Congress, other subsidies remain in place, including the RFS.

The RFS, as established by the 2007 Energy Independence and Security Act, mandates that biofuels must be mixed into the supply of America's transportation fuels. By 2022, according to the statute, there must be 15 billion gallons (56.7 billion L) of corn-based ethanol in the nation's gasoline supply (in addition to 21 billion gallons [79.4 billion L] of non-corn biofuels). "In essence," writes analyst Nicholas D. Loris, "the RFS mandates a market for corn farmers and biofuel producers . . . and artificially eliminates the risk and competition necessary for a healthy and growing economy." Loris goes on to assert that such an artificially distorted market for ethanol has created consequences, "including potential engine damage, environmental costs, food riots internationally, and higher prices."[14] Growing recognition of these and other consequences, in addition to direct costs to taxpayers, have led to calls from environmentalists, fiscal conservatives, and others to end all federal government subsidies of corn-based ethanol.

> "Billions of taxpayer dollars have been squandered on an industry that relentlessly seeks additional special interest carve-outs."[13]
>
> —Ryan Alexander, president of the nonpartisan group Taxpayers for Common Sense.

Problems with Ethanol

Problems with ethanol begin with the fuel itself. Ethanol is not as efficient as gasoline, and most car engines cannot run on pure ethanol. As of 2015 most ethanol sold in the United States is found in two blends: E10 (10 percent ethanol, 90 percent gasoline) and E85 (85 percent ethanol, 15 percent gasoline). The E85 blend can only be distributed by retrofit-

Federal Corn Ethanol Subsidies Must End

In addition to the Renewable Fuel Standard, there are numerous programs scattered within different US government agencies that provide financial aid for corn ethanol producers, refiners, and consumers. Over the past thirty-plus years billions of dollars in federal support have gone to the ethanol industry. The group Taxpayers for Common Sense, which compiled the information in this table, argues that the time has come for corn ethanol to succeed or fail in the marketplace without any government subsidies.

A Sampling of Federal Subsidies for Corn Ethanol

Program Name	Description	Total Cost 2009–2013
Bioenergy Program for Advanced Biofuels	Payments to advanced biofuels facilities to expand annual production	$55 million
Biorefinery Assistance Program	Grants and loan guarantees for advanced biofuels and for heat and power facilities	$25 million
Repowering Assistance Program	Reimbursements for biorefineries to replace fossil fuel power sources with biomass	$6.9 million
Clean Cities Program	Grants for biofuels infrastructure and promoting alternative-fuel vehicles	$300 million
State Energy Programs	Grants to states for ethanol blender pumps, ethanol promotion, and other projects	$3.1 billion (not all corn ethanol-related)
Congestion Mitigation and Air Quality Improvement Program	Grants to states and cities for transportation projects that improve air quality	$4.4 billion for 2013–2014 (not all corn ethanol-related)

Source: Taxpayers for Common Sense, "Taxpayer Supports for Corn Ethanol in Federal Legislation," April 2014. www.taxpayer.net.

ted filling stations and utilized by flex-fuel vehicles—cars with engines that have been specially designed to run on more than one type of fuel. Both E10 and E85 contain less energy as pure gasoline. In other words, they deliver fewer miles per gallon of fuel. Economics professor and ethanol critic Mark J. Perry estimates that ethanol provides 27 percent lower fuel economy than gasoline. "Consumers have to purchase more fuel to drive the same distances," he asserts, which is "why consumers are willing to search for gas stations with ethanol-free fuel."[15]

Ethanol may cause problems beyond lower efficiency. Ethanol burns hotter than petroleum-based gasoline. This may damage engines and corrode pumps, fuel lines, and injectors. Such problems may become worse if Environmental Protection Agency proposals to change the ethanol blend from E10 to E15 (15 percent ethanol, 85 percent gasoline) go forward. Car manufacturers have warned that their engine warranties might be voided if damage is caused by fuel that contains too much ethanol.

Rising Food Prices

In addition to producing inferior fuel, America's ethanol program has had a negative impact on the production of food, especially corn. Corn is a key ingredient in many foods, and America supplies 40 percent of the world's corn harvest. But supplies of corn available for food uses have tightened as more of America's corn has gone into ethanol instead. In 2000 less than 5 percent of the US corn crop was used to produce ethanol; more than 90 percent was used to feed people and livestock in the United States and other nations. By 2013 that balance had changed significantly, with 40 percent of US corn production devoted to ethanol, 45 percent used for livestock feed, and only 15 percent available for food and beverage products.

By placing limits on the amount of corn available for food uses, ethanol mandates create upward pressures on food prices that affect the consumer. "There's very little question about whether or not ethanol subsidies and related mandates, which essentially pay farmers to grow fuel instead of food, drive up the price of food," argues magazine editor Peter Suderman. He cites a 2008 Congressional Budget Office analysis that concluded that at least 10 to 15 percent of a 5.1 percent uptick in food prices over a twelve-month period was attributable to ethanol subsidies. Suderman notes that "higher food prices hit the poor the hardest" and concludes that "the ethanol mandate is essentially a tax on the poor, in the U.S. and elsewhere."[16]

Biofuels Are Not Necessary for Energy Security

Proponents of ethanol policies say that they are needed to reduce America's oil imports. However, some important things have changed since 2007, when the current RFS was created. Since then advances in deepwater drilling and, especially, shale oil extraction (fracking) have led to a dramatic surge in domestic oil production. In addition, Americans are consuming less oil and gasoline, in large part because of vehicle fuel-efficiency standards. These factors (domestic production and conservation) both dwarf ethanol's impact on energy markets and make America's dependence on imported oil a declining and less significant problem.

> "The ethanol mandate is essentially a tax on the poor, in the U.S. and elsewhere."[16]
>
> —Peter Suderman, senior editor at *Reason* magazine.

Most realistic estimates on the potential of ethanol conclude that it can only replace a small fraction of the petroleum America uses. In 2011 ethanol and biofuels accounted for only 4 percent of transportation fuel used in the United States—despite using around 40 percent of America's corn crop and costing billions of dollars in federal subsidies. "Displacing oil with ethanol may be reducing Americans' dependence on oil, but the real question is: How much reduction and at what cost?" argues Loris. "The answer is, very little reduction in oil use at a very high cost."[17]

Negative Environmental Consequences

Environmental concerns, especially the goal of reducing greenhouse gas emissions, are commonly cited to support ethanol subsidies. But the actual environmental impact of ethanol may be far worse than what was promised.

Burning ethanol also releases carbon dioxide and other greenhouse gases. Carbon pollution is supposedly mitigated by the making of biofuels because growing corn takes carbon dioxide out of the atmosphere. But the reality of ethanol belies this theory. Making ethanol can be both polluting and energy intensive. It typically involves the use of chemical fertilizers that are actually made from natural gas, which is a fossil fuel. Likewise, the use of pesticides, insecticides, and fossil fuel–powered machinery to grow, harvest, and transport corn creates greenhouse gas emissions. Many ethanol manufacturing plants burn coal or natural gas to power the distillation of corn into ethanol.

In addition, because government ethanol programs have created a demand for corn and thus a rise in corn prices, many farmers have plowed up land that had been in soil conservation programs or lying fallow, or they have converted grasslands or wetlands into cornfields. Associated Press reporters Dina Cappiello and Matt Apuzzo used satellite data to calculate that 5 million acres (2 million ha) of land set aside for conservation have been lost to corn production. The Environmental Working Group has estimated that 23 million acres (9.3 million ha) of wetlands and grasslands have been turned into cropland between 2008 and 2011—a development it attributes at least in part to government ethanol programs. These unfarmed lands were actually absorbing more carbon dioxide from the atmosphere than the cornfields that replaced them. Their conversion into farms has thus resulted in a significant net release of carbon dioxide emissions. In addition, runaway corn cultivation has strained underground water supplies, created soil erosion, and increased water pollution from chemical fertilizer runoff.

Better Energy Alternatives

There are better ways to achieve the supposed goals of corn ethanol subsidies. Government conservation programs can better reduce oil consumption. The development of hybrid, electric, and hydrogen-fueled cars offers a better path to reduced greenhouse gas emissions. An argument could be made for government support of energy sources such as solar, geothermal, or even other biofuels, but not for corn ethanol. "While the biofuels industry as a whole was intended to help achieve American energy independence, reduce greenhouse gas emissions, and spur rural economic development," concludes Alexander, "the corn ethanol industry has fallen short of achieving these goals while spurring numerous unintended consequences and long-term liabilities that have resulted in more harm than good."[18]

Chapter Two

Can Biofuels Reduce Greenhouse Gas Emissions?

Biofuels Can Help Reduce Greenhouse Gas Emissions

- Nations around the world are committing to reduce greenhouse gas emissions to prevent potentially calamitous climate disruptions.
- Fossil fuels are a main source of greenhouse gas emissions.
- While burning biofuels creates greenhouse gas emissions, the process of growing plants for biofuels takes carbon out of the atmosphere.

The Debate at a Glance

Biofuels Might Not Actually Reduce Greenhouse Gas Emissions

- Biofuels such as ethanol and biodiesel create greenhouse gas emissions when burned.
- Growing biofuel crops and turning them into fuel is energy intensive and produces carbon emissions.
- Growing biofuels can lead to the destruction of forests and other indirect land-use changes that increase greenhouse gas emissions.

Biofuels Can Help Reduce Greenhouse Gas Emissions

"Biofuels can help reduce greenhouse-gas emissions by providing an alternative to releasing fossil-fuel carbon into the atmosphere."

—*The Economist,* a British periodical on economic and business affairs.

Economist, "What Happened to Biofuels?," September 7, 2013.

Consider these questions as you read:

1. Why are countries trying to reduce greenhouse gas emissions?
2. Do you believe that measuring a crop's impact from planting to combustion adequately addresses the question of whether biofuels reduce greenhouse gas emissions? Explain your answer.
3. What is carbon sequestration? Which biofuels might work as carbon sequesters?

Editor's note: The discussion that follows presents common arguments made in support of this perspective, reinforced by facts, quotes, and examples taken from various sources.

At a United Nations (UN) summit in Lima, Peru, in December 2014, representatives from 196 nations agreed to set a general goal of reducing their greenhouse gas emissions. Greenhouse gases include carbon dioxide, methane, nitrous oxide, and other gases that trap heat in the atmosphere. Scientists warn that too much atmospheric warming because of increasing greenhouse gases could lead to food shortages, deadly storms, mass extinctions, and flooding related to rapid sea-level rise. According to a 2014 report by the UN Intergovernmental Panel on Climate Change, by the year 2050 humanity needs to reduce its greenhouse gas emissions 41 to 72 percent below 2010 levels in order to prevent catastrophic results.

Biofuels have an important place in achieving the goals of greenhouse gas reduction, especially in the transportation sector. According to the US Environmental Protection Agency (EPA), transportation accounted for 27 percent of total US greenhouse gas emissions in 2011, and it is responsible for more than half of the growth in America's greenhouse gas emissions between 1990 and 2011. The Global Renewable Fuels Alliance (GRFA) estimates that 25 to 30 percent of all greenhouse gas emissions (sometimes referred to as GHGs) come from the burning of liquid fossil fuels in autos, trains, boats, and planes. "Those [transportation-related] GHGs need to be a priority . . . [for] combating climate change," asserts GRFA spokesperson Bliss Baker. "Biofuels must be an integral part of that fight."[19] To understand why, one must know how burning fossil fuels creates excessive greenhouse gas emissions—and why biofuels are different.

The Difference Between Fossil Fuels and Biofuels

When an automobile burns conventional gasoline or diesel fuel, it is releasing energy—and carbon—that was captured by plants millions of years ago. Through photosynthesis, plants absorb radiant energy from the sun, take carbon dioxide from the atmosphere, and convert the carbon into organic material. Normally this carbon is released back into the atmosphere when the plants die and decompose; this intake and release of carbon is called the carbon cycle. Sometimes, however, plants do not decompose but are trapped underground. Petroleum and coal are created when plants are fossilized; the carbon they took from the atmosphere is buried as complex hydrocarbons. When these fossil fuels are extracted and burned for energy, the carbon that had been trapped for millions of years is released back into the atmosphere in the form of carbon dioxide and other greenhouse gases.

When an automobile burns ethanol or biodiesel instead of conventional fuels, it releases comparable amounts of greenhouse gas emissions. But instead of releasing carbon that had been stored underground for millions of years, it is releasing carbon that only recently had been removed from the atmosphere by the photosynthesis of the corn, sugarcane, or other plants grown for biofuel feedstock. In other words, producing and

The Benefits of a Carbon-Neutral Fuel

Any serious effort to halt climate change must include a reduction in greenhouse gas emissions. One key way to accomplish this is by increasing the use of biofuels. Over their life cycle, biofuels both absorb and emit greenhouse gases. That life cycle begins with the growth of plant-based feedstock; growing plants absorb the greenhouse gas carbon dioxide (CO_2) from the atmosphere. The rest of the biofuels life cycle involves production and transport of feedstock, the manufacture of biofuels from that feedstock, and finally the combustion of the fuel. However, absorption of CO_2 at the beginning of the biofuels life cycle essentially cancels out the emissions during the rest of that cycle. Because of this, unlike fossil fuels, biofuels are considered to be a carbon-neutral fuel source.

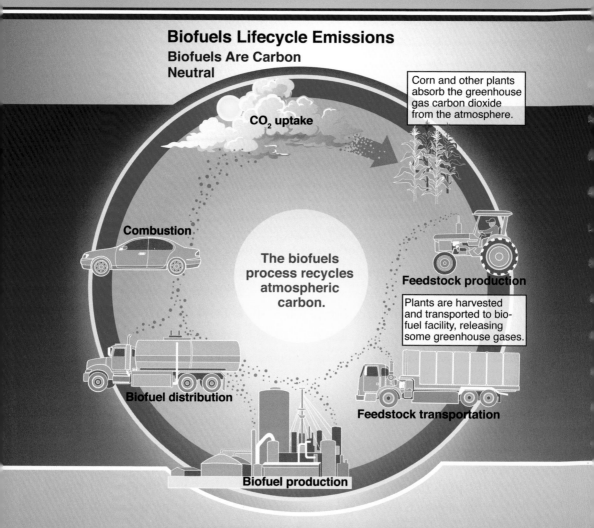

Biofuels Lifecycle Emissions
Biofuels Are Carbon Neutral

CO_2 uptake

Corn and other plants absorb the greenhouse gas carbon dioxide from the atmosphere.

Combustion

The biofuels process recycles atmospheric carbon.

Feedstock production

Plants are harvested and transported to biofuel facility, releasing some greenhouse gases.

Biofuel distribution

Feedstock transportation

Biofuel production

Source: ITEC, "Ethanol Fact: Environment," 2014. www.itecref.com.

burning biofuels creates fewer net greenhouse gas emissions over a current time frame than burning fossil fuels. "Biofuels essentially recycle atmospheric carbon,"[20] argues Geoff Cooper, vice president of the Renewable Fuels Association.

Life-Cycle Assessments

The offset is not 100 percent. Greenhouse gas emissions are produced when fertilizers and pesticides are made to help grow biofuel crops as well as when biofuels themselves are manufactured and transported. These factors need to be taken into account when calculating the potential for reducing greenhouse gas emissions by replacing petroleum fuels with biofuels. This approach of measuring a crop's impact from planting to combustion is called a life-cycle assessment.

Scientists and researchers have conducted life-cycle assessments of different biofuels and conventional fossil fuels to calculate how much greenhouse gas emissions were made from cultivation (or in the case of fossil fuels, extraction) of raw fuel material through the refining, transporting, and combustion of these fuels. These studies, according to environmental scientists Wouter M.J. Achten and Louis V. Verchot, "confirm that biofuel systems have the potential to reduce greenhouse gas emissions and fossil energy consumption."[21] The exact amount of greenhouse gas emissions that can be reduced with the use of biofuels can vary greatly depending on which biofuel feedstock is used and the processes used to grow, harvest, and convert it to biofuel.

> "Biofuels essentially recycle atmospheric carbon."[20]
>
> —Geoff Cooper, senior vice president of the Renewable Fuels Association.

Some biofuels have greater emissions-reduction potential than others. The EPA has calculated that ethanol from cornstarch produces 23 percent less greenhouse gas emissions compared to making and burning a comparable amount of gasoline from petroleum. According to the National Corn Growers Association, this figure can be improved as research advances: "Recent evidence shows multiple ways of producing ethanol with 50 percent or less GHG compared to gasoline production."[22] Sugarcane has even higher potential because it requires less pesticide and soil tillage, and more of the plant can be used for energy. The EPA has calculated that producing and burning sugarcane-based ethanol can emit 60 percent less greenhouse gases than gasoline, while the Brazilian Sugarcane Industry Association claims 90 percent greenhouse gas savings.

Biodiesel also holds promise in reducing greenhouse gas emissions. Research by the Argonne National Laboratory calculated that greenhouse gas emissions produced over the life cycle (production to consumption) of biodiesel could be 52 percent lower than the emissions of petroleum diesel. In their survey of research on biofuels and greenhouse gas emissions, Achten and Verchot found that biodiesel made from palm oil can reduce emissions by 38 to 79.5 percent compared to producing and burning a comparable amount of regular diesel. Biodiesel made from oil from the jatropha tree can reduce emissions anywhere from 49 to 72 percent, and soybean-based biofuels have an emissions reduction potential of 57 to 74 percent.

> "Recent evidence shows multiple ways of producing ethanol with 50 percent or less GHG [greenhouse gas emissions] compared to gasoline production."[22]
>
> —National Corn Growers Association, a trade group of American corn farmers.

Can Some Biofuels Sequester Carbon?

Some biofuels that are still in the development stage may even take more carbon out of the atmosphere than they emit over their life cycle. Perennial grasses such as switchgrass and miscanthus have been researched as potential biofuel feedstocks that can be converted to ethanol and other biofuels. They not only grow rapidly, but they also develop extensive root systems that can reach 30 feet (9 m) underground. This enables them to actually take carbon dioxide from the atmosphere and store it in the soil, a process called carbon sequestration. These grasses also can be cut and harvested year after year without replanting. This helps reduce greenhouse gas emissions since carbon dioxide is released from the soil to the atmosphere every time ground is plowed and replanted. The Union of Concerned Scientists has estimated that the United States has the potential to sustainably produce 400 million dry tons (362 million t) of switchgrass and similar energy crops by the year 2035. This is enough to create 32 billion gallons (121 billion L) of biofuel and reduce greenhouse gas emissions by 107 billion tons (97 billion t) a year.

The conclusion is clear. Extracting and burning fossil fuels releases carbon that has been stored underground for millions of years and is a major factor in increasing the concentration of greenhouse gases in the atmosphere. Finding replacements for fossil fuels that do not create greenhouse gas emissions is becoming an urgent necessity. Biofuels can fill that need. Because biofuel feedstock crops are renewable and remove carbon dioxide from the atmosphere at the time they are being grown, biofuels can be an indispensable tool in the challenge of meeting the world's energy needs while reducing greenhouse gas emissions.

Biofuels Might Not Actually Reduce Carbon Emissions

"After all the inputs and land-use changes are considered, biofuels often lead to greater greenhouse gas emissions and worse pollution."

—David Kreutzer, an energy and defense analyst with the Heritage Foundation.

David Kreutzer, "Great Green Fleet = Big Red Ink," Daily Signal, July 24, 2013. www.dailysignal.com.

Consider these questions as you read:

1. What problems do critics have with the idea that biofuels are carbon neutral? Are these concerns justified? Explain your answer.
2. Why are fertilizers a significant issue with regard to greenhouse gas emissions?
3. What are indirect land-use changes and how do they affect whether biofuels reduce greenhouse gas emissions?

Editor's note: The discussion that follows presents common arguments made in support of this perspective, reinforced by facts, quotes, and examples taken from various sources.

Many countries are promoting the use of biofuels because of concerns about greenhouse gas emissions. The burning of fossil fuels—such as the combustion of gasoline or diesel fuel in automobile engines—releases significant amounts of greenhouse gases into the atmosphere. Proponents claim that using biofuels instead of gasoline or diesel may help nations reduce overall greenhouse gas emissions.

This is not because biofuels burn cleaner, however. They contribute just as many greenhouse gas emissions as fossil fuels when combusted. Rather, it is because plants from which biofuels are made remove carbon dioxide from the atmosphere. In theory, at least, biofuels are carbon neutral. That is, from planting to combustion the plants used for biofuels remove as many greenhouse gases from the atmosphere as they emit.

That is the theory. The reality is far different. In practice, the production and development of biofuels does little to reduce greenhouse gas emissions. Several factors contribute to this disappointing outcome. The production of biofuels creates direct greenhouse gas emissions even prior to their combustion. The use of fertilizer to grow biofuel crops such as corn increases emissions of nitrous oxide, another greenhouse gas. In addition, efforts to make more biofuels often lead to land-use changes such as deforestation, a significant contributor of greenhouse gas emissions. The ultimate benefit of substituting biofuels for fossil fuels in terms of reducing greenhouse gas emissions is questionable.

Farming and Transportation

One reason for this has to do with the process of growing biofuel feedstocks. During the growing period significant amounts of carbon dioxide and other greenhouse gases are emitted. Modern high-yield agriculture relies on nitrogen-based synthetic fertilizers such as ammonia. Many of the leading crops for biofuels, such as corn in the United States, are typically grown with such fertilizers. The manufacture of ammonia fertilizer typically requires the burning of coal or natural gas. Possibly even more troubling is the fact that carbon dioxide (CO_2) is a by-product of that manufacturing process. "Even high-efficiency ammonia plants are heavy CO_2 emitters: two tons are released for every ton of ammonia produced,"[23] according to science writer Celeste LeCompte. In addition, the application of ammonia and other nitrogen fertilizers not only stimulates plant growth but also stimulates the growth of soil bacteria that consume the nitrogen in the fertilizer and release nitrous oxide—a greenhouse gas almost three hundred times more efficient at trapping heat than carbon dioxide.

Growing the biofuel feedstock is just part of the process that makes ethanol and biodiesel available at the pump. The crops have to be transported to processing plants, physically transformed into usable biofuels, and transported to filling stations and other distribution sites. All these steps use energy and create significant greenhouse gas emissions.

False Assumptions About Biofuels

The idea that biofuels reduce greenhouse gas emissions is built on false assumptions. It is often assumed, for instance, that emissions created by burning biofuels are negated by absorption of carbon dioxide as biofuel crops grow. However, this is only true if the plant growth would not have happened otherwise. Often, biofuels crops simply replace food crops. This illustration compares gasoline and biofuels in a scenario where crops previously used for food are instead used for biofuels. Because there is no new plant growth, there is no additional greenhouse gas absorption, and thus no greenhouse gas reduction benefit.

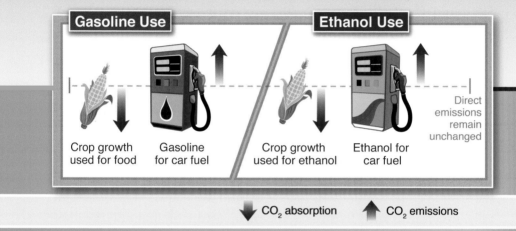

Source: Tim Searchinger and Ralph Heimlich, "Avoiding Bioenergy Competition for Food Crops and Land," World Resources Institute, January 2015. www.wri.org.

Biofuels and Land-Use Change

In addition to the direct greenhouse gas emissions associated with biofuels, one must also consider the impact of biofuels agriculture on the land itself. "Land-use change (LUC) occurs when land is converted to biofuel feedstock production from other uses or states, including non-feedstock agricultural lands, forests, and grasslands,"[24] writes biofuels scientist Jennifer B. Dunn. Changing a land's use may significantly alter its greenhouse gas emissions. Forests are generally carbon sinks, meaning they remove carbon from the atmosphere and store it in wood. Biofuel crop plants often do not absorb as much carbon from the atmosphere as forest or wetland plants. Changing a carbon-rich forest or wetland to a biofuel plantation can significantly increase the overall level of greenhouse gas emissions produced in the area.

Biofuels can also cause such land-use changes indirectly. If farmland is used to grow energy crops and biofuel feedstocks, the land is not available for food and animal feedstock. Because of this dynamic, argues climate researcher Bjørn Lomborg, "it is likely that biofuels cause net increase in CO_2 emissions, because they force agriculture to cut down forests elsewhere to grow food."[25] Such indirect land-use change caused by biofuels is harder to calculate than direct land-use change, but it is no less real in its impact on greenhouse gases.

The Global Effect of US Policies

A well-studied example of indirect land-use change created by biofuels can be seen in the impact of US biofuel mandates. As American farmers devote more and more of their production to biofuel feedstocks such as corn and soybeans, less food is available for export to other countries. The United States is a significant food exporter; drops in exports can force nations to increase their own food production by converting forests and grasslands into farmland. The resulting deforestation and land-use change creates an effective increase of carbon dioxide and other greenhouse gases in the atmosphere.

Scientists at Duke University have used computer modeling to examine just this scenario and to assess how biofuels and biofuels policy can affect greenhouse gas emissions not only in the United States but also around the world. In a 2013 paper they concluded that because of deforestation and fertilizer use, increasing America's mandates on biofuels "leads to increases in global greenhouse

> "It is likely that biofuels cause net increase in CO_2 emissions, because they force agriculture to cut down forests elsewhere to grow food."[25]
>
> —Bjørn Lomborg, a statistician, author, and former director of the Environmental Assessment Institute.

gas emissions that exceed the reductions in U.S. fossil fuel emissions,"[26] reports journalist Dan Haugen. In other words, gains in lowering greenhouse gas emissions in the United States (burning less fossil fuel) are canceled out by increases abroad (due primarily to land-use changes such as deforestation). "If you think that the ethanol mandate is a big winner in terms of its greenhouse gas implications, it doesn't appear to be,"[27] said Brian Murray of Duke University, one of the paper's authors.

Palm Oil and Peatlands

A similar dynamic can be seen with palm oil, a cheap and popular source for biodiesel. In a report produced by Friends of the Earth and other environmental organizations, Indonesian activists Bondan Andriyanu and Laili Khairnur assert that "biofuels are the main driver of faster growth in demand for vegetable oil worldwide—demand which is largely met by expansion of new palm oil plantations, as this is the cheapest vegetable oil."[28] To meet this demand, much of Indonesia's arable land has been turned over for biofuel farming. This, in turn, has led many farmers to burn or convert peatlands and tropical forests into farms— another example of indirect land-use change (ILUC). Converting forests and peatland into farmland, whether for biofuel crops or for food farming operations displaced by biofuel plantations, disturbs the soil and releases significant greenhouse gas emissions.

> "If you think that the ethanol mandate is a big winner in terms of its greenhouse gas implications, it doesn't appear to be."[27]
>
> —Brian Murray, director of the Environmental Economics Program at Duke University's Nicholas Institute for Environmental Policy Solutions.

Peatlands are a special concern in Indonesia and elsewhere. Peatlands, including swamps, bogs, and tundra, have thick layers of waterlogged soil consisting of dead and decaying plant material. This plant material consists of carbon that has been taken from the atmosphere. The water prevents the soil from decomposing and releasing carbon dioxide back to the atmosphere. Indeed, the world's peatlands store twice as much carbon as the trees in the world's forests. But when peatlands are drained for farmland, their organic materials are exposed to air, leading to decomposition and the release of carbon dioxide. Trapped methane—a potent greenhouse gas—is also released when peatlands are converted to farmland. Andriyanu and Khairnur conclude that, "when impacts of ILUC are accounted for, biodiesel that originates from palm oil, soybean, or rapeseed has more carbon emissions than fossil diesel."[29]

Biofuel mandates may originate from the best of intentions to prevent global warming. But because of land-use changes and other factors, a growing number of scientists have reached the conclusion that biofuels are no panacea for reducing greenhouse gas emissions, and in some cases may make the problem worse. Nations trying to reduce their greenhouse gas emissions should be cautious in embracing biofuels as a solution.

Chapter Three

Does Biofuels Development Threaten Global Food Production?

Biofuels Development Is a Threat to Global Food Production

- Food crops such as corn and soybeans, which are used to make biofuels, are not available as food.
- Growing crops for biofuels takes up land, water, and resources that could be used for food production.
- People in poor countries are most likely to be victimized by converting farms to biofuel plantations.
- Food should have higher priority than fuel.

The Debate at a Glance

Biofuels Development Does Not Threaten Global Food Production

- Farmers can grow enough crops for both food and biofuel demands.
- Producing biofuels often creates food and animal feed as a by-product.
- Biofuels should not be blamed for higher food prices.
- The food versus fuel argument against biofuels does not justify abandoning biofuels.

Biofuels Development Is a Threat to Global Food Production

"Burning hundreds of millions of tonnes of staple foods to produce biofuels is a crime against humanity."

—Jean Ziegler, former United Nations investigator.

Jean Ziegler, "Burning Food Crops to Produce Biofuels Is a Crime Against Humanity," *Guardian*, November 26, 2013. www.theguardian.com.

Consider these questions as you read:

1. Which specific examples and statistics best support the argument that biofuels create food shortages and hunger? Explain your answer.
2. What emotions are evoked by critics who frame biofuels as a food versus fuel conflict?
3. How compelling is the argument that food production is threatened when both food and nonfood crops are used for biofuels? Explain your answer.

Editor's note: The discussion that follows presents common arguments made in support of this perspective, reinforced by facts, quotes, and examples taken from various sources.

In recent years many countries have enacted policies to encourage the production of biofuels such as ethanol and biodiesel. Such fuels are supposed to create a sustainable and environmentally friendly substitute for petroleum-based fuels. In Europe, for example, 10 percent of transportation fuels are supposed to consist of biofuels and other renewable energy sources by 2020. To meet this demand, countries around the world have made biofuel crops such as sugarcane and palm oil important export industries. However, as biofuel production has ramped up, serious questions have emerged.

41

A leading concern is the relationship between biofuels and the ongoing and serious problem of world hunger. Many of the world's valuable biofuel crops are also food staples. Observers have questioned whether the devotion of more and more resources to biofuels has impacted the ability of the world's farmers to produce enough food to meet a growing population and whether consumers (especially in poor countries) are being harmed. Jean Ziegler, a United Nations official charged with protecting humanity's right to food, frames this as both a moral issue and an issue of priorities. "Almost all biofuels used in Europe are made from crops, such as wheat, soy, palm oil, rapeseed and maize, that are essential food sources for a rapidly expanding global population," he writes. "Europe now burns enough food calories in fuel tanks every year to feed 100 million people."[30] Ziegler and others argue that rich nations should prioritize feeding people over making biofuels.

> "Because ethanol competes for corn with food and animal feed, it has a direct impact on the cost of food."[31]
>
> —Timothy Wise, policy research director at Tufts University's Global Development and Environment Institute.

Corn and Food Prices

A close examination of two popular biofuels—ethanol and biodiesel—reveals that both have potentially severe impacts on food production. The most common source of ethanol is corn, a staple food crop. Corn is not only used in many food products (including chips and cereals) but also provides animal feed in the production of pork, beef, and poultry. However, US ethanol policies now take around 40 percent of America's corn harvest—roughly 15 percent of the world's corn production. Researchers have calculated that the amount of annual ethanol production in the United States in 2011 (almost 14 billion gallons [60 billion L]) represents enough corn to feed 570 million people for a year.

Removing that much corn from food markets creates tighter supplies and ultimately higher prices. "Because ethanol competes for corn with food and animal feed, it has a direct impact on the cost of food,"[31] argues

Sustainable Food Future Is Unlikely with Crop-Based Biofuels

According to researchers at the World Resources Institute, a global target of producing enough biofuel to meet 10 percent of the world's transportation needs would, by 2020, use up the equivalent of 20 percent of the 2010 world food harvest. By 2050, a 10 percent biofuels target may create food shortages and increase the likelihood of world hunger.

2010 Food Crop Production

Needed to Meet 10% Biofuels Target in 2020

Needed to Meet 10% Biofuels Target in 2050

Source: Tim Searchinger and Ralph Heimlich, "Avoiding Bioenergy Competition for Food Crops and Land," World Resources Institute, January 2015. www.wri.org.

Timothy A. Wise, the policy research director for the Global Development and Environment Institute. In addition to affecting the price of corn itself, ethanol mandates affect the supplies and prices of other staple crops because farmers have switched to growing corn for ethanol instead. The price of meat, eggs, and dairy products are also impacted by higher animal-feed costs. In 2008 the prices of many food crops doubled; a review of the price spikes by the National Academy of Sciences concluded that 20 to 40 percent of the price increase was due to global biofuels expansion.

Biodiesel and Food Production

Another biofuel that has gained popularity is biodiesel, which can be used in diesel engines in cars and other machines. Biodiesel is derived from plant oils or animal fats. Biodiesel has been touted as a good way to recycle used vegetable cooking oil, for example. However, the mass production of biodiesel (due largely to government mandates in the United States and Europe) has also negatively impacted global food production.

Although biodiesel can be made from a variety of sources, popular feedstock sources are soybean oil, palm oil, and rapeseed (canola). Soy is an important food crop, and vegetable oils including palm oil are commonly used in food products or for cooking. As in the case of corn, using soy and other plants for biofuels instead of food results in smaller food supplies and higher prices. One study estimated that biofuel mandates in Europe could increase prices of cooking vegetable oil by 36 percent, corn prices by 22 percent, sugar prices by 21 percent, and wheat prices by 13 percent.

Mandates for biodiesel production have also had an indirect impact on food production as land previously used for growing food is converted into biofuel feedstock plantations. *New York Times* journalist Elisabeth Rosenthal has examined how the market for biofuels has impacted food and hunger in the Central American nation of Guatemala, where many farms and ranches have been converted into plantations that grow sugarcane and palm oil. "Guatemala's lush land, owned by a handful of families, has proved ideal for producing raw materials for biofuels," writes Rosenthal. "Suchitepéquez Province, a major corn-producing region five years ago, is now carpeted with sugar cane and African palm."[32]

Across the globe in Indonesia, millions of acres have been converted into industrial plantations harvesting palm oil. In many cases, lands have been seized from local people. "Whether by legal or illegal means, many companies are driving their plantations into areas where communities have farmed communally-held land for . . . generations," writes

Indonesian activist Laili Khairnur. "Indonesia's forests are crucial for providing food for local communities (through gathering, growing and hunting). . . . The conversion of these forests to plantations for biofuels . . . threaten[s] the food sovereignty of those who rely on them most."[33] Similar instances of land grabs have happened in Africa and other places where land has been taken for biofuel feedstock plantations.

Water and Land Issues

Another way that biofuel production impacts food production is through its use of freshwater supplies. An estimated 11.8 trillion gallons (45 trillion L) of water was used to irrigate biofuel farms in 2007—about six times the amount that humans drank that year. Some of this water could have been used to grow food instead. In Brazil and Central America, growing sugarcane to produce the biofuel ethanol can take large amounts of water. Rosenthal reports that small-scale farmers in Guatemala are hurt by biofuel plantations that "divert and deplete rivers to feed industrial scale irrigation systems."[34] A plan to convert more than 74,000 acres (30,000 ha) in Mozambique to sugarcane production will take irrigated water previously used by local farmers to grow food crops. In Paraguay, families living next to large soy plantations have had to deal with local well failures and water shortages, making farming nearly impossible.

> "The conversion of [Indonesia's] forests to plantations for biofuels . . . threaten[s] the food sovereignty of those who rely on them most."[33]
>
> —Laili Khairnur, an author and social activist.

Even if the plants grown for biofuels are not food (such as switchgrass), cultivating them still takes water, land, and resources that could otherwise be used to grow food for hungry populations. The jatropha tree has been touted for many years as a promising biodiesel crop that is drought resistant and can grow on marginal lands. The African nation of Uganda has developed an aggressive foreign-financed biofuels development program in which thousands of acres of jatropha trees have been planted—with some negative results on food production. "Biofuels now compete for the small land plots that were once used to grow food," notes Wise. He calculates that 1 acre (0.4 ha) of land growing 430 jatropha trees is needed to produce a single year's worth of biodiesel for one car. To produce a small fraction of the fuel necessary to power Uganda's six hundred thousand cars "means hundreds of thousands of hectares of fertile land must be used to produce jatropha rather than food."[35]

Food Is More Important than Fuel

Wise calls on the Ugandan government "to prioritize food security over biofuels" and its farmers "not to abandon food crops completely in favor of biofuel crops."[36] He and other critics of biofuels mostly agree that climate change is a real issue and that alternatives to burning fossil fuels should be pursued. But they argue that biofuels are not the ideal alternative energy source, as long as people continue to be hungry from lack of food. "The consumption of fossil fuels must be rapidly reduced," concedes Ziegler, "but solutions lie with the reduction of energy consumption, public transportation and alternative sources of clean energy, not land-using biofuels with so many detrimental consequences."[37]

Biofuels Development Does Not Threaten Global Food Production

"Classifying food vs. fuel as a debate gives it more credit than it deserves. It is actually a myth manufactured by the oil industry and trumpeted by anti-ethanol zealots."

—Ryan Buck, a corn and soybean farmer and the president of the Minnesota Corn Growers Association.

Ryan Buck, "Food vs. Fuel 'Debate' Falls Apart," *Star Tribune*, September 21, 2014. www.startribune.com.

Consider these questions as you read:

1. Do you agree with critics that it is wrong to frame the biofuels debate as a food versus fuel question? Why or why not?
2. What importance is attached to the by-products of biofuels production, and why?
3. Should the views of corn farmers be considered biased when examining biofuels? Why or why not?

Editor's note: The discussion that follows presents common arguments made in support of this perspective, reinforced by facts, quotes, and examples taken from various sources.

Biofuels have come under attack in recent years due to the question of food versus fuel. The most common biofuel feedstocks used at present are plants rich in starches, sugars, and oils—plants that are also grown for food. This leads some to question whether using these plants for fuel rather than for food is a good idea in an era when hunger remains a serious global problem. The biofuels industry has been blamed for reduced grain stocks, high food prices, hunger, and other social problems. Some hunger activists have called for ending all government mandates for the production of biofuels.

However, most food versus fuel arguments against biofuels fall apart under closer scrutiny. Promoting biofuels need not cause decreases in food production. Biofuels are not necessarily responsible for hunger or higher food prices. Finally, ongoing advances in technology and the development of new plant and waste sources for biofuels make the food versus fuel question even less relevant. The important environmental and other benefits of biofuels should not be sold short because of misleading arguments about their role in global food supplies.

Corn Production

Much criticism of biofuels focuses on corn, which is used both for food and the biofuel ethanol. The United States is the world's leading corn producer. In recent years much of the corn grown in the United States (around 40 percent) has been turned into ethanol to meet government renewable fuel mandates.

However, that does not mean there is not enough corn left for food. Farmers in the United States and other countries can grow enough corn and other crops to meet both food and fuel demands. American farmers have been especially productive. According to official US government estimates, the 2014 corn crop came close to a record 14.5 billion bushels, half a million bushels more than 2013's record harvest. The amount of corn produced per acre has risen from 39.4 bushels in 1954 to 167.4 in 2014.

In addition to growing productivity, an important point to remember is that converting crops into biofuels does not destroy all their food value. The fermentation and distillation process that converts the starches and sugars of corn into ethanol also creates a protein-rich by-product called distiller's dried grains with solubles (DDGS). These grains can be used as animal feed for cattle, pigs, and chickens. Livestock feed was and remains the largest single market for US corn; only a small percentage of corn is directly eaten by humans.

When factoring in productivity and DDGS, the impact of ethanol on the food markets is negligible. In 2000, before the ethanol industry took off, the United States produced 9.9 billion bushels of corn, out of which 5.2 billion were used for livestock feed. In 2013 almost 5 billion bushels

The graph pairs annual data on food price inflation with the amount of corn used to make ethanol and ethanol by-products. Contrary to claims that diverting corn from food to energy uses would tighten food supplies and raise food prices, the data does not show an obvious correlation between corn use for ethanol and higher food costs.

Annual Food Price Inflation Rates vs. Corn Use for Ethanol & Co-Products

Corn Use for Ethanol/Co-products
Annual Food Price Inflation

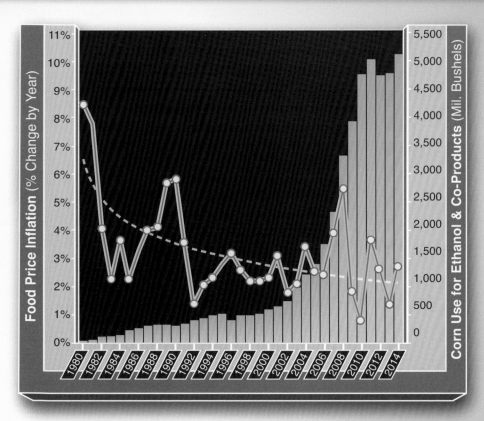

Source: Renewable Fuels Association, "Corn Prices Are Plunging, So What About Retail Food Prices?," September 2014. www.ethanolrfa.org.

were diverted for ethanol. However, the combination of a larger overall harvest (13.9 billion bushels) due to greater efficiencies and acres planted, and the 1.1 billion bushels of DDGS produced by the ethanol industry meant that more livestock feed was produced by corn farmers in 2013 than in 2000. "Despite what the doubters say," argues Minnesota corn farmer Ryan Buck, "we grow more than enough corn for food and fuel."[38]

Protein for Animals

The confluence of biofuels and protein production can be seen in other crops. Soybeans are often pressed for oil that can then be made into biodiesel, another important biofuel. As with corn, the process of making biofuels produces a protein-rich food by-product. "Biodiesel actually has a positive impact on soybean meal supplies," according to the American Soybean Association. "Processing biodiesel from soybeans using only the oil, which comprises 20% of the soybean, and leaves the other 80% available as protein-rich soy meal for use as animal feed, thus creating a surplus and bringing down the cost of feed."[39]

> "Despite what the doubters say, we grow more than enough corn for food and fuel."[38]
>
> —Ryan Buck, corn farmer.

Biofuel production complements food production. According to the World Bioenergy Association, global production of biofuels from corn, soybeans, rapeseed, and cereals produced more tons of protein feed than tons of biofuel. Additionally, protein feed created by sugarcane ethanol production nearly matched the amount of ethanol produced.

Biofuels Are Not to Blame for Higher Food Prices

Many critics of biofuels blame the use of corn in fuel production for creating food shortages and higher corn crop prices, which in turn are blamed for higher food prices for consumers. Their criticisms are unfounded. For one, there is no apparent connection between ethanol production and corn prices. In 2008 corn prices peaked at over $7.50 a bushel, a development some blamed on the 9.3 billion gallons (35 billion L) of ethanol produced that year. In 2014, however, corn prices hovered around $3.80 a bushel—even though ethanol production was on track to produce 13.9 billion gallons (52.6 billion L).

But even if ethanol production could be shown to create higher corn prices, that does not necessarily translate into higher food prices. "In truth, fluctuations in corn prices do not significantly affect consumer food prices," according to an analysis of prices by the Renewable Fuels Association. "This is true even for food items for which corn is a major input, like cereals, snack foods, meat, milk, and eggs."[40] This is in part because crop prices account for only 14 percent of the cost of a food item at the grocery store. The remaining 86 percent comes from packaging, marketing, processing, transport, and other expenses.

> "Biofuels should not be blamed for price increases in Sub-Saharan Africa."[41]
>
> —Pangea, a bioenergy promotion group.

While crop prices can have a greater impact on higher food prices in developing nations, biofuels are not necessarily to blame. In Africa, for instance, other factors that contribute to food prices include the cost of oil, growing populations, and production constraints due to lack of agricultural infrastructure. "Biofuels should not be blamed for price increases in Sub-Saharan Africa," according to Pangea, a bioenergy promotion group. "They should be promoted as opportunities to stabilize local agricultural production"[41] by providing energy, animal feed, reduced reliance on oil, and additional markets for farmer's crops.

Nonfood Biofuel Sources

In addition to corn and soy, biofuels can be made from plants that are not grown as food crops. Promising research and development projects have explored the ethanol potential of a variety of nonfood sources, including different types of grasses. One of these is switchgrass, a grass that can grow 10 feet (3 m) tall and is native to American prairies. Another potential biofuel feedstock, miscanthus, or elephant grass, is a reed that is native to Asia. One advantage of grass crops is that they can be used on marginal farmland. Lands that are too saline, prone to flooding or drought, or with soil quality too poor to efficiently grow corn and other food crops could be utilized for grasses instead, thereby sidestepping the food versus fuel debate entirely.

Biodiesel also has the potential to be made from nonedible plant sources. One that has received much attention is the jatropha tree, a tropical tree that produces seeds with high oil content. Jatropha can be grown on marginal land, consumes less fertilizer and water than other plants, and is resistant to most pests. India, Mexico, Mali, and Uganda are among the nations that have promoted jatropha as a biofuel source. Other sources being investigated for biodiesel production are algae (plant-like microorganisms that grow in water), and recycled animal fats that are by-products of meat processing.

A Misguided Attack

Taking all of these factors into account—productivity, protein feed by-products, and the development of biofuel feedstocks other than food crops—there is enough land and agricultural productivity worldwide for both food and fuel. Biofuels are an important tool in the vital effort to reduce use of fossil fuels and reduce greenhouse gas emissions. They should continue to be supported against misleading arguments that try to create a false choice between making fuels and feeding the world. We can do both. Bob Dinneen, president of the Renewable Fuels Association, is right when he says that "the food vs. fuel argument is just another misguided attack on biofuels."[42]

Chapter Four

Are Biofuels Essential for National Security?

Biofuels Are Essential for National Security

- America's military and economy are overly dependent on a single commodity: oil.
- Much of America's oil comes from unfriendly foreign regimes.
- Technologies can be developed to create biofuels that can readily replace petroleum-based fuels.
- Having biofuels as an alternative defuses the threat of oil price shocks that create problems for America's economy and defense budget.

The Debate at a Glance

Biofuels Are Not Essential for National Security

- Biofuels are an inferior source of energy compared with petroleum-based fuels.
- The United States can easily supply its military petroleum needs from domestic sources.
- Biofuels are more expensive than fossil fuels and are a misallocation of resources.
- Other alternatives to petroleum, such as converting coal to liquid fuel, are a better option than biofuels.

Biofuels Are Essential for National Security

"Winning the race to develop . . . biofuels will enhance our nation's security by adding a new source to our diverse supply of fueling sources and by reducing our reliance on imported oil."

—Daniel Poneman, deputy secretary of energy under President Barack Obama.

Quoted in *Hill*, "Feds Invest in Biofuels for the Navy," September 19, 2014. http://thehill.com.

Consider these questions as you read:

1. What different levels of American oil dependence are described? Which do you believe is most important, and why?
2. What does Secretary of the Navy Ray Mabus mean when he suggests that alternative fuels have become a matter of saving lives? Do you agree or disagree with the connection he makes?
3. What arguments are made in response to the claim that biofuels are too expensive compared to regular fuels? Are they persuasive? Why?

Editor's note: The discussion that follows presents common arguments made in support of this perspective, reinforced by facts, quotes, and examples taken from various sources.

The argument that biofuels play an important role in American national security can be summed up as follows: the US military—and the United States in general—relies heavily on fuel made from a single commodity—petroleum, or oil. This dependence on oil-based fuels has several serious ramifications impacting military operations and overall national security. By developing biofuels as a replacement or alternative for oil, the United States can mitigate or prevent these potential harms to national security.

America's Dependence on Oil

America's dependence on petroleum exists on several different levels. One is in America's military operations. The US Department of Defense is the single-largest consumer of petroleum-based fuels in the world. America's military depends on petroleum to fuel its tanks, vehicles, ships, and airplanes. Airpower is especially dependent on oil since airplanes require liquid fuels.

The importance of fuel to America's military was highlighted by recent US campaigns in Iraq and Afghanistan. Military operations require fuel, and soldiers stationed in remote areas need convoys to supply them. A study by the Marine Corps found that one marine was killed or wounded for every fifty convoys that supplied fuel and water to troops fighting in Afghanistan. "Cutting fuel means fewer convoys and fewer casualties," argues Secretary of the Navy Ray Mabus. "Diversifying energy supplies doesn't just save money, it saves lives."[43]

Oil and the Global Economy

However, America's dependence on oil goes well beyond what is directly consumed by the military. The United States as a whole needs around 19 million barrels of oil a day to meet its needs and to keep its economy functioning. Seventy-one percent of that oil consumption is for transportation needs. America's oil dependency is but part of a growing global thirst for oil. Interruptions in the supply of oil could cause the global economy to stumble or even collapse—and take America's economy with it.

America's oil dependency is complicated by the fact that the United States gets much of its oil from other countries. The United States contains only about 3 percent of the world's oil reserves, and it produces less oil than it uses. In 2012 America relied on net imports (imports minus exports) of oil products for 40 percent of the oil it consumed. "America depends on oil to a dangerous degree," argues military veteran and biofuels advocate Michael Breen, "and we do not produce enough of it here at home to ensure our future security or prosperity."[44]

> "Diversifying energy supplies doesn't just save money, it saves lives."[43]
>
> —Ray Mabus, US secretary of the navy.

The Harms of Oil Dependence

America's oil dependence has several ramifications for national security. One is the effect of oil prices. Oil price increases can hamper defense readiness since dollars spent on fuel cannot be spent on training, equipment, personnel, and other necessities. Between 2005 and 2011 military fuel costs rose 381 percent ($4.5 billion to $17.3 billion). "Over this period," writes security analyst Andrew Holland, "fuel consumption actually declined by 4%, but that was overcome by a surge in oil prices."[45]

Every $1 rise in a barrel of oil costs the US Navy and Marine Corps an extra $30 million per year.

Oil price increases and swings harm the broader US economy as well. "The American economy relies on an uninterrupted supply of low-cost oil (which is dependent on the global market)," argues Holland. "As such the U.S. military must defend shipping lanes around the world."[46] For example, the United States spends an estimated $90 billion a year and places thousands of military personnel in harm's way to protect the Strait of Hormuz. This is a narrow stretch of water at the entrance of the Persian Gulf where much of the world's oil is produced and shipped. While only a small portion of that oil goes directly to the United States, cutting off that chokepoint would have dire effects on the global oil market and create economic havoc throughout the world.

> "America depends on oil to a dangerous degree, and we do not produce enough of it here at home to ensure our future security or prosperity."[44]
>
> —Michael Breen, a retired US Army captain and the director of the Truman National Security Project.

Drilling for More Oil Is Not a Solution

Some argue that American oil production is making a comeback with new shale oil extraction, and they believe America can meet its demands with more drilling. However, this argument fails to take into consideration the fact that oil is a global commodity and oil markets are tightly interlinked. The United States simply cannot drill enough oil to insulate

Biofuels Protect Military from Changing Oil Prices

The US military is heavily dependent on oil for operating its tanks, trucks, ships, and aircraft all over the world. Because of this the military is vulnerable to price fluctuations, which can be significant (as can be seen in the graph). Establishing biofuels as an alternative to oil protects the military from uncertainties and potentially damaging disruptions caused by changing oil prices.

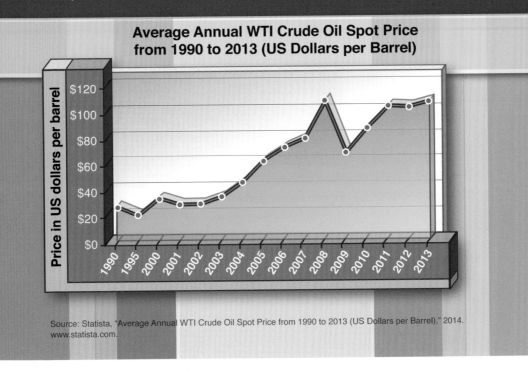

Average Annual WTI Crude Oil Spot Price from 1990 to 2013 (US Dollars per Barrel)

Source: Statista, "Average Annual WTI Crude Oil Spot Price from 1990 to 2013 (US Dollars per Barrel)," 2014. www.statista.com.

itself from oil price fluctuations or international supply disruptions that could harm American consumers and America's economy. Even if the United States became self-sufficient in oil in the near future, it would not solve national security concerns, according to Mabus. "Self-sufficiency will not insulate the United States against oil price shocks. . . . It will not lessen global political and economic friction from resource competition or threats to infrastructure and distribution."[47]

Developing Alternative Fuels

If simply drilling for more oil does not solve the problem, what can be done? Military leaders have concluded that the United States must develop alternatives to petroleum—and biofuels are an obvious alternative. The military has tried out biofuels from a variety of feedstocks. Most, if not all, can be produced domestically, thus ensuring American control over its own energy supplies. These raw materials for biofuels include algae, waste animal fats like beef tallow, vegetable oils like soy and palm oil, and even municipal waste.

Technology has been successfully developed to convert these feedstocks into "drop-in" diesel or jet fuel. This refers to fuel that can be directly used in ships and airplanes without any modifications in engines or in the infrastructure used to transport them. Such fuels have already been successfully used to power military ships and airplanes. In 2014 military contracts were awarded for three biofuel companies to produce 100 million gallons (378.5 million L) of jet and diesel fuel from biofuels. The US Navy and Air Force plan to get at least 50 percent of their fuel needs from biofuels and other nonpetroleum fuels by the year 2020.

The Cost Is Worth It

Critics of these fuel goals often note that biofuels are generally much more expensive than conventional fuels. They contend that the added expense of using biofuels is unjustified and even harmful to national security. However, they fail to grasp the idea that price alone cannot dictate national security decisions; taking control over one's energy sources can be worth the higher costs. "There have always been critics who challenge every new idea . . . as too costly or too risky," argues Mabus. "But our first mission must be to protect our nation by assuring stability around the globe. If concerns over cost and fear of change had carried the day, we would still be using sails."[48]

Furthermore, the military has a long record of helping new products and technologies, ranging from steel to microchips, find uses in the civilian world. Military journalist Fred Kaplan notes that "some of modern history's most revolutionary products started out as too expensive; and they would have stayed that way—they might never have got off the ground—had the federal government not created the market."[49] This development could be repeated for biofuels, as prices have fallen in recent years. Prioritizing biofuels as a national security interest and investing in them not only gives the navy and other military branches more options besides oil to fuel their operations but also could help establish a vital domestic biofuels industry. Creating and sustaining such an industry "would reduce America's dependence on oil and increase our national security over the long run,"[50] concludes Holland.

Biofuels Are Not Essential for National Security

"Biofuels are counterproductive to national energy security."

—John E. Gay, a commander and public affairs officer for the US Navy.

John E. Gay, "Can Biofuels Accelerate Energy Security?," *Joint Force Quarterly,* iss. 73, 2nd quarter, 2014. http://ndupress.ndu.edu.

As you read, consider the following questions:

1. In what ways are biofuels inferior to fossil fuels? What part should this play in the national security debate?
2. How expensive are biofuels? How do their costs affect national security?
3. What alternatives besides biofuels exist to replace petroleum-based fuels? What are their potential advantages and disadvantages?

Editor's note: The discussion that follows presents common arguments made in support of this perspective, reinforced by facts, quotes, and examples taken from various sources.

In recent years there has been a concerted effort by some US politicians and military leaders to promote biofuels as a tool to enhance national security. Their argument is that America's dependency on oil threatens the country's national security. Their proposed solution is that the United States—and, more specifically, America's military—should actively promote and develop biofuels as an alternative to oil-based fuels.

But are biofuels truly the indispensable solution to national security? While reliance on petroleum-based fuels may be a long-term problem for the United States, biofuels are not necessarily the solution. A rigorous examination of biofuels reveals that they are not an adequate replacement for fossil fuels. What's more, policies favoring biofuels over other energy sources are costly and may ultimately harm American security interests. There are better ways to approach the problem of oil dependency than biofuels.

Why Biofuels Are Inferior to Fossil Fuels

Biofuels are not a new technology; they have been around almost as long as the automobile. Early automobiles and tractors used biofuel, and the first American commercial cellulose ethanol plant dates to 1910. However, US naval officer John E. Gay notes that "biofuels production declined over time because it was expensive, inefficient, and unsustainable."[51] The disadvantages that led to biofuels being replaced by petroleum-based fuels remain to this day.

One disadvantage is that biofuels contain less energy density than petroleum-based fuels. Ethanol contains 33 percent less energy than gasoline; biodiesels contain 8 percent less energy than petroleum diesel. This has direct and negative ramifications on how the military operates. Greater volumes of fuel are needed to accomplish given tasks and missions. The potential real-life impact of biofuels can be seen in recent US military campaigns. The logistics of conveying fuel to US troops in Afghanistan and Iraq consumed a major part of US military missions there. Fuel convoys were a frequent target of enemy attacks. Gay argues that "the use of biodiesel . . . may increase the risks and number of casualties due to its reduced energy density, which will require more fuel to accomplish the same mission."[52]

In addition, biofuels in some cases have been found to be more corrosive to metal than regular diesel fuel. Biodiesel is more susceptible than regular diesel to biodegradation caused by microbes that over time can create corrosive acids. This can cause problems with maintenance and readiness, especially as the average age of navy ships grows because fewer new ships are being built. Military analysts Brian Slattery and Michaela Dodge argue that the "use of fuels with potentially harmful consequences is a recipe for a fleet readiness crisis"[53] that would jeopardize national security interests.

Biofuels Are Costly

Finally, biofuels are much more expensive than conventional fuel. A 2014 report by the Government Accountability Office found that the Pentagon paid $150 per gallon for jet fuel made from algae at a time when a gallon of conventional jet fuel cost $2.88. Not all biofuels are that expensive, but they consistently cost more to procure than petroleum-based fuel. For example, the navy spent $26 a gallon for biofuels for naval exercises in 2012. This would be price competitive with oil—if oil ever sold for $1,000 a barrel (which it has not). Actual oil prices rarely top $100 a barrel. "There is just no rational explanation of how spending on biofuel this expensive can actually improve national security,"[54] argues energy analyst Thomas J. Pyle.

The costs of biofuels have raised concerns over whether spending the extra money on these fuels takes away resources from other critical military programs or national security needs. John McCain, a US senator from Arizona and former navy fighter pilot, is among those who believe that pursuing military biofuels is a costly and misguided endeavor. In a 2012 letter to Secretary of the Navy Ray Mabus, McCain said the decision to purchase 450,000 gallons (1.7 million L) of biofuels at a cost of $26 per gallon for a demonstration was "a terrible misplacement of priorities" that misallocated money from training and other readiness programs. "That wasteful purchase," McCain wrote, "and the Navy's commitment of $170 million to develop a commercial biofuels refinery, will result in a real cost to the readiness and safety of our Sailors and Marines."[55]

"The Navy's commitment of $170 million to develop a commercial biofuels refinery, will result in a real cost to the readiness and safety of our Sailors and Marines."[55]

—John McCain, a Republican US senator for Arizona and a former navy pilot.

Supporters of biofuels argue that these fuels can help protect America's military and economy from oil price volatility and disruptions in oil supplies. However, biofuels also face significant price and supply challenges. Much of the energy in biofuel crops stems from chemical fertiliz-

Costly Biofuels Take Money from Other Military Needs

Biofuels are far more expensive than conventional fuels. Whereas conventional diesel fuel can be procured for around $3.60 a gallon by the US military, compatible biodiesel can cost $26 a gallon. The price difference harms national security, some argue, by using up funds that could be better spent in other areas.

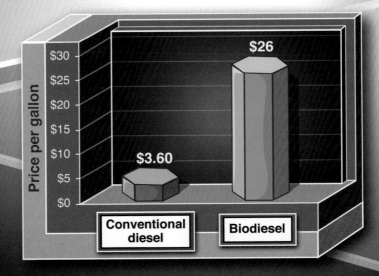

Source: Brian Slattery and Michaela Dodge, "Biofuel Blunder: Navy Should Prioritize Fleet Modernization over Political Initiatives," *Issue Brief* 4,054, Heritage Foundation, September 24, 2013. www.heritage.org.

ers derived from fossil fuels, tying biofuel prices to oil prices. In addition, the agricultural commodities that are a source of biofuel feedstock are, like oil, also subject to global price shocks and supply disruptions due to bad weather and other causes.

Stresses on Natural Resources

Competing for oil can be a source of conflict between nations, something biofuel proponents often point out. However, by promoting biofuels as a possible replacement for oil, the United States just may be swapping one wellspring of resource conflict for another. Growing biofuel crops requires large amounts of land—land that would potentially be used for food agriculture, commercial forestry, textile crops, or urban expansion. Biofuel production also requires large quantities of freshwater—another potential flashpoint for resource conflicts.

Military experts such as Gay have voiced concerns over whether producing biofuels on a scale necessary to displace petroleum may place too much stress on global natural resources and create regional conflicts that may result in calls for US military intervention. "Biofuels mandates in Europe and the United States pressure agricultural expansion and stress natural resources," Gay argues. "These practices are detrimental to energy security and could require U.S. military involvement in countries where there is currently little security threat."[56]

> "Our own oil production is a better, cheaper source for defense fuel security."[57]
>
> —David Kreutzer, an economist and energy analyst.

Alternatives to Biofuels

Instead of costly and resource-consuming biofuels, the American military can and should promote different national security solutions on the problem of oil dependency. One is to make America's own domestic oil production a priority. Supporters of biofuels often argue that the United States needs to develop its own energy sources and not rely on foreign nations. But the United States is still a leading oil producer and can easily provide enough fuel for its military needs. America's defense operations use about 360,000 barrels of oil a day. But while that seems like a large number, it is actually small compared to total world oil production of 90 million barrels per day. American oil production is predicted to top 10 million barrels a day in 2015. "Our own oil production is a better, cheaper source for defense fuel security," concludes energy and economics analyst David Kreutzer. "The military will get the oil it needs even if we were entirely cut off from foreign sources."[57] Kreutzer and others argue that opening more land and sea areas to drilling and encouraging shale oil extraction will ensure that America's energy needs are met.

Another solution is energy conservation and efficiency. Investing in fuel-efficient technologies, lighter materials, and energy-use reduction strategies can reduce the amount of liquid fuels needed and enhance energy security for military operations.

Finally, biofuels are not the only alternative energy sources to petroleum. Technologies exist that can create high-quality diesel and jet fuel from both coal and natural gas. The United States has plentiful reserves of both of these established fossil fuels as well as established infrastructure to exploit them. Tapping these resources can better address the problem of national energy security than pursuing costly biofuels.

Source Notes

Overview: Biofuels

1. Quoted in Diane Cardwell, "Military Spending on Biofuels Draws Fire," *New York Times,* August 27, 2012. www.nytimes.com.
2. Quoted in Cardwell, "Military Spending on Biofuels Draws Fire."
3. Bliss Baker, "Global Ethanol Production to Reduce GHGs by over 106 Million Metric Tons in 2014," May 21, 2014. www.ethanolrfa.org.
4. Quoted in Roddy Scheer and Doug Moss, "Ethanol's Unrealized Promise," *E—the Environmental Magazine,* September 13, 2014. www.emagazine.com.

Chapter One: Should the US Government Continue to Support Ethanol Production?

5. John R .Block, "Renewable Fuels Benefit Entire Economy," *Orange County Register,* October 28, 2013. www.ocregister.com.
6. George W. Bush, "Bush Delivers Speech on Renewable Fuel Sources," *Washington Post,* April 25, 2006. www.washingtonpost.com.
7. Pam Johnson, "Ethanol Requirements Are Good, Not Bad, for America's Economy," Fox News, September 20, 2013. www.foxnews.com.
8. Block, "Renewable Fuels Benefit Entire Economy."
9. Delayne Johnson, "Renewable Fuels Standard Spurred Ethanol Breakthroughs,*" Des Moines Register,* September 14, 2014. www.desmoinesregister.com.
10. Saskatchewan Eco Network, "Why Is Ethanol a 'Green Fuel?'" http://econet.ca.
11. Renewable Fuels Association, "Ethanol Facts: The Environment," March 2014. www.ethanolrfa.org.
12. Bruce Dale, "Renewable Energy, Not Just a Nice Idea," *StarTribune,* October 7, 2012. www.startribune.com.
13. Ryan Alexander, "Good News for Corn, Bad News for You," *U.S. News & World Report,* March 12, 2014. www.usnews.com.
14. Nicholas D. Loris, "The Ethanol Mandate: Don't Mend It, End It," *Heritage Foundation Backgrounder,* no. 2,811, June 12, 2013. www.heritage.org.
15. Mark J. Perry, "Consumers Don't Want Ethanol," *Hill,* September 28, 2013. http://thehill.com.
16. Peter Suderman, "Want Cheaper Food? End the Ethanol Mandate," *Reason,* February 27, 2013. http://reason.com.
17. Loris, "The Ethanol Mandate."
18. Alexander, "Good News for Corn, Bad News for You."

Chapter Two: Can Biofuels Reduce Greenhouse Gas Emissions?

19. Quoted in Global Renewable Fuels Alliance, "Biofuels Are the Answer to Reducing Global Transport GHG Emissions," December 9, 2014. www.globalrfa.org.

20. Geoff Cooper, "Busting Big Oil Myths on the RFS and Ethanol, Part III: ILUC and Greenhouse Gases," Energy Collective, June 5, 2013. http://theenergycollective.com.

21. W.M.J. Achten and L.V. Verchot, "Implications of Biodiesel-Induced Land-Use Changes for CO_2 Emissions," *Ecology and Society*, vol. 16, no. 4, 2011. http://dx.doi.org.

22. National Corn Growers Association, "Ethanol Offers Growing Environmental Benefits," Delta Farm Press, April 10, 2013. http://deltafarmpress.com.

23. Celeste LaCompte, "Fertilizer Plants Spring Up to Take Advantage of U.S.'s Cheap Natural Gas," *Scientific American*, April 25, 2013. www.scientificamerica.com.

24. Jennifer B. Dunn et al., "Land-Use Change and Greenhouse Gas Emissions from Corn and Cellulosic Ethanol," *Biotechnology for Biofuels*, April 10, 2013. www.biotechnologyforbiofuels.com.

25. Bjørn Lomborg, "Climate Change Is a Problem. But Our Attempts to Fix It Could Be Worse than Useless," *Telegraph*, November 3, 2014. www.telegraph.co.uk.

26. Dan Haugen, "Study: U.S. Biofuels Policy Pushes Greenhouse Gas Emissions Overseas," Midwest Energy News, March 28, 2013. www.midwestenergynews.com.

27. Quoted in Haugen, "Study."

28. Laili Khairnur, "Briefing: Indonesia on the Front Line," Friends of the Earth Europe, 2012. www.foeeurope.org.

29. Khairnur, "Briefing."

Chapter Three: Does Biofuels Development Threaten Global Food Production?

30. Jean Ziegler, "Burning Food Crops to Produce Biofuels Is a Crime Against Humanity," *Guardian*, November 26, 2013. www.theguardian.com.

31. Marie Brill and Timothy A. Wise, "Fiddling in Rome While Our Food Burns," *Aljazeera*, October 17, 2013. www.aljazeera.com.

32. Elisabeth Rosenthal, "As Biofuel Demand Grows, So Do Guatamala's Hunger Pangs," *New York Times*, January 5, 2013. www.nytimes.com.

33. Khairnur, "Briefing."

34. Rosenthal, "As Biofuel Demand Grows, So Do Guatamala's Hunger Pangs."

35. Timothy A. Wise, *Fueling the Food Crisis: The Cost to Developing Countries of US Corn Ethanol Expansion*, ActionAid USA, 2012. www.actionaidusa.org.

36. Wise, *Fueling the Food Crisis.*
37. Ziegler, "Burning Food Crops to Produce Biofuels Is a Crime Against Humanity."
38. Ryan Buck, "Food vs. Fuel 'Debate' Falls Apart," *StarTribune*, September 21, 2014. www.startribune.com.
39. American Soybean Association, "Biodiesel Backgrounder," July 2014. www.soygrowers.com.
40. Renewable Fuels Association, "Corn Prices Are Plunging, So What About Retail Food Prices?," September 2014. www.ethanolrfa.org.
41. Pangea, "Myths and Facts About Bioenergy in Africa," 2012. www.pangealink.org.
42. Quoted in Renewable Fuels Association, "Food vs Fuel Debunked (Again)," September 8, 2014. www.ethanolrfa.org.

Chapter Four: Are Biofuels Essential for National Security?

43. Ray Mabus, "Green Water," *Foreign Policy*, August 6, 2013. http://foreignpolicy.com.
44. Michael Breen, "Why the Fight over the 'Great Green Fleet' Is Fuelish," *Time,* July 12, 2012. www.time.com.
45. Andrew Holland, *Advanced Biofuels & National Security*, American Security Project, January 2013. www.americansecurityproject.org.
46. Holland, *Advanced Biofuels & National Security.*
47. Mabus, "Green Water."
48. Mabus, "Green Water."
49. Fred Kaplan, "Why We Need a Greener Military," *Slate,* May 18, 2012. www.slate.com.
50. Holland, *Advanced Biofuels & National Security.*
51. John E. Gay, "Can Biofuels Accelerate Energy Security?," *Joint Force Quarterly,* iss. 73, 2nd quarter, 2014. http://ndupress.ndu.edu.
52. Gay, "Can Biofuels Accelerate Energy Security?"
53. Brian Slattery and Michaela Dodge, "Biofuel Blunder: Navy Should Prioritize Fleet Modernization over Political Initiatives," Heritage Foundation, September 24, 2013. www.heritage.org.
54. Thomas J. Pyle, "The Navy's Use of Biofuels Is Inefficient and Costly," *U.S. News*, July 19, 2012. www.usnews.com.
55. John McCain, US Senate website, "Letter from Senator McCain to Navy Secretary Ray Mabus Regarding Biofuels," July 27, 2012. www.mccain.senate.gov.
56. Gay, "Can Biofuels Accelerate Energy Security?"
57. David Kreutzer, "Great Green Fleet = Big Red Ink," Daily Signal, July 24, 2013. www.dailysignal.com.

Biofuels Facts

Ethanol

- Ethanol, also called ethyl or grain alcohol, is made by processing and fermenting the sugars and starches in plants.
- The United States and Brazil are the world's leading producers of ethanol, accounting for 84 percent of the world's ethanol in 2013.
- As of the beginning of 2015, all gasoline sold in Brazil must consist of at least 25 percent ethanol. Eighty-eight percent of vehicles on Brazilian roads have flexible fuel engines that can run on any mixture of gasoline and ethanol.
- The plants used to make ethanol vary by region. In the United States 96 percent of ethanol produced is derived from corn. In Brazil sugarcane is used to make ethanol. In Europe ethanol is made from wheat and sugar beets.
- Ethanol also can be made from cellulosic plant material such as cornstalks, plant residues, grasses, and waste wood chips. However, making ethanol from cellulose is more difficult as energy and processing is required to break down the hard plant material into usable sugars.
- According to the World Resources Institute, making ethanol from sugarcane converts around 0.5 percent of the solar radiant energy absorbed by the plant into ethanol energy. Corn-based ethanol contains 0.15 percent of the solar energy absorbed by the corn.

Biodiesel

- Biodiesel is made from vegetable oil, fats, or greases.
- Vegetable oils and other fats are modified through a process known as transesterification; the resulting biodiesel has lower viscosity and boiling point than straight vegetable oil, which is not recommended as a vehicle fuel.
- Biodiesel can be sold and burned either straight or blended with conven-

tional petroleum-based diesel. The most common blends in the United States are B5 (5 percent biodiesel) and B20 (20 percent biodiesel).

- According to the US Energy Information Administration, the United States produced 1.3 billion gallons (4.9 billion L) of biodiesel in 2013; as of December 2014 America had the capacity to produce 2.1 billion gallons (8.3 million L) annually.
- As of 2014 there were 138 biodiesel production plants in the United States.

Climate Change and Greenhouse Gas Emissions

- Gases that create a greenhouse effect in the atmosphere include carbon dioxide, methane, and nitrous oxide.
- From 1990 to 2013, energy-related carbon dioxide emissions in the United States increased by about 0.3 percent per year; 92 percent of these emissions come from the combustion of fossil fuels.
- The transportation sector accounts for 34 percent of America's energy-related carbon dioxide emissions.
- At a November 2014 summit in China, President Barack Obama announced that the United States was setting a target of reducing greenhouse gas emissions by 28 percent below 2005 levels.
- Some global climate scientists argue that the world's nations need to reduce greenhouse gas emissions by 80 percent below 1990's levels by the year 2050 to prevent disastrous climate change.

US Government Policies on Biofuels

- The Renewable Fuel Standard (RFS) was authorized by the 2007 Energy Independence and Security Act.
- The Environmental Protection Agency (EPA) administrates and enforces the RFS. Every year the EPA specifies how many gallons of corn ethanol and other biofuels must be blended into the nation's fuel supply.
- The 2013 EPA rule mandates that 16.55 billion gallons (62.6 billion L) of the nation's fuel supply (9.74 percent of the total) consist of renewable fuels. Of this number, at least 2.75 billion gallons (10.4 billion L) must come from advanced biofuels.

- According to the EPA, an advanced biofuel must attain a 50 percent reduction in greenhouse gas emissions over its life cycle relative to conventional gasoline. Biodiesel qualifies as an advanced biofuel. Corn-derived ethanol is excluded from this category, but ethanol from other sources (such as Brazilian sugarcane) may be included.
- By 2022 the US transportation fuel supply is supposed to include 36 billion gallons (136 billion L) of biofuels, of which no more than 15 billion gallons (56.8 billion L) would be corn ethanol. Sixteen billion gallons (60.5 billion L) are supposed to come from cellulosic sources; few observers expect this particular goal to be achieved.

Biofuels in the Military

- Since 2012 the US Air Force has required all of its planes be able to fly with a 50/50 blend of biofuel and conventional fuel.
- Both the US Air Force and Navy have set a 2016 goal of having at least 50 percent of aviation and other liquid fuels come from alternative fuel sources, including biofuels.
- In fiscal year 2011 the Department of Defense consumed 117 million barrels of oil at a cost of $17 billion.
- Three-quarters of the American military's energy use is so-called operational energy, which is used for training, moving, and sustaining military forces.
- The air force accounts for more than half (53 percent) of the American military's use of petroleum. The navy makes up 28 percent of total military fuel consumption, the army 18 percent, and the Marines Corps and the Coast Guard less than 1 percent.

Related Organizations and Websites

Advanced Biofuels Association
800 Seventeenth St. NW, Suite 1100
Washington, DC 20006
website: www.advancedbiofuelsassociation.com

The Advanced Biofuels Association represents more than forty companies involved in the making of cellulosic and other advanced drop-in biofuels. It supports public policies that enable sustainable advanced biofuels to compete with petroleum-based fuels. Its website includes information on the different technologies and feedstocks used to make biofuels.

Alternate Fuels Data Center (AFDC)
website: www.afdc.energy.gov

Part of the US Department of Energy's Clean Cities Initiative, the AFDC website provides up-to-date information to help consumers and decision makers reduce petroleum consumption through the use of biofuels and other alternative fuels. It includes information on biofuels prices, locations of refueling stations, and federal, state, and local regulations and incentives.

Biofuelwatch
e-mail: biofuelwatch@ymail.com • website: www.biofuelwatch.org.uk

A nonprofit organization based in Great Britain with operations in the United States, Biofuelwatch seeks to provide information on industrial biofuels and their harms related to climate change, the environment, and human rights. Its website provides links to reports and articles on biofuels.

Corn for Food Not Fuel!

website: www.cornforfoodnotfuel.com

The website, sponsored by the American Meat Institute and other food-industry organizations, provides graphics and news links that make the case that corn-based ethanol has negative repercussions for food supplies and prices.

Fuel Freedom Foundation

18100 Von Karman Ave., Suite 870
Irvine, CA 92612
phone: (949) 833-6960 • fax: (949) 833-6940
e-mail: action@fuelfreedom.org • website: www.fuelfreedom.org

The Fuel Freedom Foundation is a nonprofit organization that seeks to end America's dependency on oil and make ethanol and other biofuels more widely available to consumers. It produced the movie *Pump*, which is viewable on its website.

Renewable Fuels Association (RFA)

425 Third St. SW, Suite 1150
Washington, DC 20024
phone: (202) 289-3835 • fax: (202) 289-7519
website: www.ethanolrfa.org

The RFA is a trade association for the US ethanol industry. It provides information on ethanol and energy policy for governments and the general public, and it works to expand the market for corn-based ethanol. Its website includes articles, infographics, videos, and links on ethanol and biofuels.

Union of Concerned Scientists

2 Brattle Sq.
Cambridge, MA 02138-3780
phone: (617) 547-5552 • fax: (617) 864-9405
website: www.ucsusa.org

The Union of Concerned Scientists is a nonprofit advocacy organization. It seeks to develop, promote, and implement practical solutions to climate change and other pressing global problems. It supports research into biofuels from nonfood crops and improving farming techniques and management practices to make biofuels truly sustainable. Reports, including *The Billion Gallon Challenge: Getting Biofuels Back on Track,* are available on its website.

US Energy Information Administration (EIA)
1000 Independence Ave. SW
Washington, DC 20585
phone: (202) 586-8800
e-mail: InfoCtr@eia.gov • website: www.eia.gov

The EIA, part of the US Department of Energy, is responsible for collecting and disseminating statistical and other information on energy production, consumption, and policies. Its website provides updated data tables and background articles on biofuels and other energy sources.

World Resources Institute (WRI)
10 G St. NE, Suite 800
Washington, DC 20002
phone: (202) 729-7600 • fax: (202) 729-7610
website: www.wri.org

The WRI is a global research organization with offices in several countries that seeks to develop ways to sustainably manage the earth's natural resources. It has issued several reports questioning the long-term sustainability and the environmental benefits of biofuels.

For Further Research

Books

Robert C. Brown and Tristan R. Brown, *Why Are We Producing Biofuels?* Ames, IA: Brownia LLC, 2012.

Joy Clancy, *Biofuels and Rural Poverty.* New York: Routledge, 2013.

Carol Hand, *Biomass Energy.* Minneapolis: ABDO, 2013.

Carla Mooney, *What Is the Future of Biofuels?* San Diego: ReferencePoint, 2013.

Ashok Pandey et al., eds, *Biofuels from Algae.* Amsterdam: Elsevier, 2014.

Robert Pool et al., *The Nexus of Biofuels, Climate Change, and Human Health.* Washington, DC: National Academies, 2014.

Frank Rosillo-Calle and Francis X. Johnson, eds., *Food versus Fuel: An Informed Introduction to Biofuels.* New York: Zed, 2011.

Periodicals

David Biello, "Scientists Tweak Photosynthesis in Pursuit of Better Biofuel," *Scientific American,* January 2012.

James A. Corlett, "It's Not So Easy Being Green," *Proceedings Magazine,* November 2014.

Feedstuffs, "Making Ethanol Sans Corn: Stanford Scientists Discover Novel Way to Make Ethanol Without Corn or Other Plants," April 21, 2014.

Hot Rod, "Is Ethanol Eating Your Carb?," August 2014.

T.A. "Ike" Kiefer, "Energy Insecurity: The False Promise of Liquid Biofuels," *Strategic Studies Quarterly,* Spring 2013.

Nature, "Fuelling the Future," vol. 502, October 17, 2013.

Andrew Steer and Craig Hanson, "Biofuels Are Not a Green Alternative to Fossil Fuels," *Guardian* (Manchester), January 29, 2015.

Peter Suderman, "Awful Ethanol: Biofuels, Busted," *Reason,* August/September 2014.

Julia Whitty, "My Heart-Stopping Ride Aboard the Navy's Great Green Fleet," *Mother Jones,* March/April 2013.

Internet Sources

Laura Barron-Lopez, "EPA Punts on Renewable Fuels Mandate Decision," *Hill,* November 21, 2014. http://thehill.com/policy/energy -environment/225002-epa-punts-final-2014-renewable-fuel-mandate.

Carl Engelking, "Biofuel Made from Corn Waste Less 'Green' than Gasoline," *D-brief* (blog), April 22, 2014. http://blogs.discovermagazine .com/d-brief/2014/04/22/biofuel-made-from-corn-waste-less-green -than-gasoline.

National Geographic Society, "Biofuels at a Crossroads," 2015. http:// environment.nationalgeographic.com/environment/energy/great-energy -challenge/biofuels.

Of Schemes and Memes (blog), "2013 Lindau Video: Fuelling Controversy," Nature.com, September 27, 2013. http://blogs.nature.com/ofsc hemesandmemes/2013/09/27/2013-lindau-video-fuelling-controversy.

Bryan Walsh, "Even Advanced Biofuels May Not Be So Green," *Time*, April 21, 2014. http://time.com/70110/biofuels-advanced-environment -energy.

Index

Note: Boldface page numbers indicate illustrations.

About the Author

William Dudley is a substitute teacher and writer whose works include *Antidepressants* and *Thinking Critically: Stem Cell Research*. He holds a BA in English from Beloit College. He lives in San Diego, California.